Implementing OpenShift

A fast-paced, practical guide for using OpenShift to
deploy your own open source Platform-as-a-Service

Adam Miller

BIRMINGHAM - MUMBAI

Implementing OpenShift

First published: October 2013

Production Reference: 1171013

Published by Packt Publishing Ltd.
Livery Place
35 Livery Street
Birmingham B3 2PB, UK.

ISBN 978-1-78216-472-2

www.packtpub.com

Cover image by Aashish Variava (aashishvariava@hotmail.com)

Credits

Author
Adam Miller

Reviewers
André Dietisheim
Daniel Kinon

Acquisition Editor
Vinay Argekar

Commissioning Editor
Harsha Bharwani

Technical Editors
Novina Kewalramani
Anita Nayak

Copy Editors
Dipti Kapadia
Gladson Monteiro
Sayanee Mukherjee
Kirti Pai

Project Coordinator
Romal Karani

Proofreader
Joanna McMahon

Indexer
Mehreen Deshmukh
Priya Subramani

Graphics
Yuvraj Mannari
Abhinash Sahu

Production Coordinator
Kirtee Shingan

Cover Work
Kirtee Shingan

About the Author

Adam Miller is currently employed at Red Hat Inc. as the Release Engineer for OpenShift Online, Red Hat's auto-scaling Platform-as-a-Service (PaaS) for applications. Adam has completed Bachelor's of Science in Computer Science and Master's of Science in Information Assurance and Security, both from the Sam Houston State University. He is a Red Hat Certified Engineer (Cert# 110-008-810), and is an active member of the open source community with a running history of contributions to the Fedora Project (FAS account name: `maxamillion`).

Acknowledgments

First, I would like to thank my family—my mother Kim, father John, stepfather Jim, stepmother Veronica, stepsister Elizabeth, mother-in-law Kathy, father-in-law Kevin and my grandparents, Bill and Mary-Jo—for their support in my writing of this book and in everything I pursue. I would also like to thank the entire OpenShift Team at Red Hat. They are the ones who've made OpenShift a reality and therefore made this book a possibility. In particular, I'd like to thank those in the team who have been invaluable mentors to me: Mike McGrath, Thomas Wiest, and Dan McPherson. I want to thank a dear friend of mine, Kyle Derr, who has been a technical mentor over the years and has helped me substantially reach a place that has made this book a possibility. I would like to thank the community members of `#rhel` on `irc.freenode.net` for the sanity checking and the technical guidance that they have provided over the years. I would also like to thank Rob Marti for hiring and mentoring me while I was at Sam Houston State University, this was largely a catalyst for what I didn't know at the time would become the career I could only have hoped for. I would like to thank Thomas Cameron for being a mentor, a motivator, and someone who provided guidance to my endeavors that ultimately lead me to writing this book. Finally, I want to thank my wife Amanda, the love of my life and primary source of inspiration in everything I do, technical or otherwise. Without her support, this book and many other wonderful occurrences in my life surely would not have happened.

About the Reviewers

André Dietisheim was quite passionate about coding Assembly Language on Commodore Amiga as a teenager. This fervor made him contribute later to the Java open source community in general and the Eclipse platform in particular.

Today, he works on JBoss Tools, the Eclipse-based tooling that Red Hat Inc. provides. He has also worked with Red Hat Inc. and his current task is to create Eclipse tooling and a Java client for OpenShift.

Daniel Kinon has been in the IT industry for 14 years and working with computers for much longer. Coming up through the ranks of Systems Administration, Daniel's passion has always been focused on automation to meet the ever-growing demands that software puts on infrastructure. Having experienced first hand the difficulties inherent in implementing PaaS, the release of OpenShift was a welcomed addition to Daniel's IT tool belt and proved extremely useful during his time working for Red Hat Inc. as a Sr. Technical Account Manager. Today, Daniel is continuing to explore the relationship between software demands and infrastructure scalability as the DevOps Architect for MarketLive Inc., the leading provider of omni-channel eCommerce technology and services. When he's not at the office or tinkering with Linux, Daniel is a husband, father, electronics hobbyist, and home brewer.

I've never seen proof of anyone succeeding on their own; I've always been baffled by those who would want to. I'd like to thank my family and mentors for always believing in me, and helping me to shape and hone my ideas and opinions, making me who I am today. And a special thank you to my wife and daughter for their support, inspiration, and smiles.

www.PacktPub.com

Support files, eBooks, discount offers and more

You might want to visit www.PacktPub.com for support files and downloads related to your book.

Did you know that Packt offers eBook versions of every book published, with PDF and ePub files available? You can upgrade to the eBook version at www.PacktPub.com and as a print book customer, you are entitled to a discount on the eBook copy. Get in touch with us at service@packtpub.com for more details.

At www.PacktPub.com, you can also read a collection of free technical articles, sign up for a range of free newsletters and receive exclusive discounts and offers on Packt books and eBooks.

http://PacktLib.PacktPub.com

Do you need instant solutions to your IT questions? PacktLib is Packt's online digital book library. Here, you can access, read and search across Packt's entire library of books.

Why Subscribe?

- Fully searchable across every book published by Packt
- Copy and paste, print and bookmark content
- On demand and accessible via web browser

Free Access for Packt account holders

If you have an account with Packt at www.PacktPub.com, you can use this to access PacktLib today and view nine entirely free books. Simply use your login credentials for immediate access.

Table of Contents

Preface

When web developers traditionally came up with their next big idea, before they could start writing any serious amount of code, they either had to deploy and run their own infrastructure or had to submit a request to their system administration team. This process would generally require some amount of budgetary approval for computer hardware, storage, network allocation, space in a rack in their organization's data center, as well as electrical, heating, and cooling considerations.

Now, with the widespread adoption of virtualization technologies, much of this process can be expedited, but there is still the administrative overhead of configuration and administration of the backend services needed to support the development environment. This is where the innovation of the cloud comes in, not just marketing buzz words that we all know and love, but real innovation that is changing the shape of IT as we know it.

For those innovative minds looking to build the next big web application or adventuring into a new web startup endeavor, these are real concerns that need addressing. This is precisely the subject area where OpenShift aims to be the answer. OpenShift is an open source PaaS (Platform as a Service) Cloud from Red Hat, Inc. OpenShift is an application platform that enables developers to not worry about the backend infrastructure, but instead worry about what they want to worry about, that is writing code to bring to life the brilliant web application they've dreamed up.

OpenShift allows developers to access infrastructure technologies, such as web servers, powering their favorite frameworks, in their favorite programming languages, and using their favorite database backend. OpenShift, at the time of writing, officially supports Perl, Python, PHP, Ruby, Java, and Node.js, along with a pairing of MySQL, PostgreSQL, and MongoDB, which can all be utilized, along with autoscaling that will dynamically respond to application load. OpenShift also offers integration with Jenkins CI, RocksMongo, PHPMyAdmin, and a feature set that is continuously growing. All of this can be controlled by either a web console, IDE integrations, or from a set of command-line tools that are available for Linux, Mac, and Windows. Deployment of code is handled by a popular version control system named Git (`http://git-scm.com/`).

What this book covers?

As previously discussed, OpenShift is an open source platform, like a Service Cloud environment, from Red Hat, Inc. OpenShift is not only a platform offering the features listed in the previous text, but is also an open source project that has devised three subprojects differing in the way they deliver the OpenShift technology to the users, developers, and community members. Further, we would know about the relationship between the subprojects, each of which has been described as follows:

- **OpenShift Origin**: It is an upstream open source project that is filed under the Apache License 2.0, and it is where all the rapid innovation of the platform happens and is targeted to be community powered and driven. The source code is listed on GitHub under the OpenShift Origin page, which is `https://github.com/openshift/`. It contains all the quickstarts, developer tools, client utilities, as well as the server code that powers the platform, which lives under the origin-server Git repository. OpenShift Origin also hosts a web presence with a multitude of information, available at `http://openshift.github.io/`. At the time of writing, OpenShift Origin is an official feature of the community-driven Fedora Project's GNU/Linux distribution; for more information please reference `https://fedoraproject.org/wiki/OpenShift_Origin`.

- **OpenShift Online**: It is the online hosted version of OpenShift; it is a hardened and stabilized version of the OpenShift Origin codebase. OpenShift Online provides users with a working OpenShift environment to utilize for free, in what is known as the "free tier", and the free offering that is now free will always be free as per the OpenShift Online documentation. There is also a commercialized offering of OpenShift Online, allowing for the purchase of extra resources when they are needed or desired, as per the OpenShift Online Pricing Guide (`https://www.openshift.com/products/pricing`). The online version will be discussed in detail, covering how to use OpenShift, because it is a great way to get up and run for free with minimal startup effort.

- **OpenShift Enterprise**: It is the Enterprise open source PaaS that allows customers to get a hardened and stabilized version of the OpenShift Origin code that is fully supported by Red Hat. This product is available for deployment on premises in the customer's own data center or private cloud. OpenShift Enterprise also features integration with Red Hat's JBoss Middleware platform. This product is available at the time of writing but will not receive further discussion throughout this book because it does not fit into the scope of this text, and anyone who is interested in this product should pursue more information at the product's web page, that is, `https://www.openshift.com/products/enterprise`.

Chapter 1, Understanding the Essentials, discusses what the cloud really is, what it means for technologists, and demystifies the new realm of acronyms, such as Infrastructure as a Service (IaaS), Platform as a Service (PaaS), and Software as a Service (SaaS). We will also go through an introductory session dedicated to the Git and SSH technologies, as they are part of the OpenShift toolset that both end users (WebDevs) and administrators (DevOps) will need to have some familiarity with. Finally, we will perform a bird's eye overview of the OpenShift architecture, covering different components of OpenShift itself.

Chapter 2, Using OpenShift, covers all the different ways for WebDevs to consume OpenShift using different approaches. We will explore the command-line utilities, the OpenShift web console (including an overview of what OpenShift calls "Quickstart Applications"), as well as IDE integrations, where we walk through using JBoss dev tools that is based on the very popular Eclipse IDE (`http://www.eclipse.org/`).

Chapter 3, OpenShift – Technologies and Working, discusses the technologies OpenShift leverages to provide its unique architecture. We will cover Pluggable Authentication Modules (PAM), Security Enhanced Linux (SELinux), Linux kernel Control Groups (Cgroups), Software Collections (SCL), and the Marionette Collective (MCollective). Once background knowledge has been established about building blocks, we will spend time discussing each component of the architecture previously introduced in *Chapter 1, Understanding the Essentials*. This section will include the OpenShift Broker, Node, Web Console, and the OpenShift REST API.

Chapter 4, Deploying an OpenShift PaaS, is mostly going to interest those who are in the DevOps arena and are interested in deploying OpenShift Origin to host their own PaaS. Here, we're going to introduce the Fedora Project and its relationship with OpenShift Origin. There will be an introduction to some open source virtualization technologies that will be used for demonstration purposes and can be used to follow along, or your virtualization technology of choice can be used. We will briefly discuss the topic of configuration management and orchestration, including an introduction to the open source Ansible IT orchestration engine (`http://www.ansibleworks.com/`); from there we will discuss methods of deploying your own OpenShift Origin environment, including a walk through using what is known as an Ansible "Playbook". Finally, we will show how to interact with your newly deployed OpenShift Origin environment just as you would with the OpenShift Online hosted service.

What you need for this book

There is a certain level of prerequisite knowledge expected; you should either be a web developer, well versed in your web framework of choice, or a little knowledge of the Git version control system would be preferred, but it will be covered in some capacity later on, so if Git is not high on the reader's skill list, fret not. For those who continue on to the DevOps portion of the text, please be aware that an introductory understanding of GNU/Linux administration is expected with preference for Red Hat Enterprise Linux or Fedora Linux administration, as these will receive focus in the instructional sections. However, the functionality of the platform will be covered at length in its own right, so explicit understanding of Red Hat and/or Fedora is not a hard requirement.

 For those who are not running Red Hat Enterprise Linux (`https://www.redhat.com/products/enterprise-linux/`) but prefer one of the "RHEL Clones", such as CentOS (`https://www.centos.org/`) or Scientific Linux (`https://www.scientificlinux.org/`), the instructional portion of this book will be fully applicable and should function just fine.

Who the book is for?

This book is for web developers in search of a development platform that offers an easier way to deploy and develop their web applications. OpenShift provides this using industry standard technology upon a flexible platform that offers the ability to write code the way the developer wants without any vendor lock-in. This book will also branch into the DevOps territory and touch on deploying the upstream OpenShift Origin codebase in a simple configuration to show how OpenShift makes life easier, not only for developers but also for those who manage the infrastructure upon which these developers depend.

Conventions

In this book, you will find a number of styles of text that distinguish between different kinds of information. Here are some examples of these styles, and an explanation of their meaning.

Code words in text are shown as follows: "Gear using the `quota` command without actually entering into an interactive shell session remotely."

A block of code is set as follows:

```
#!/usr/bin/env ruby

puts "Hello world!"
```

Any command-line input or output is written as follows:

```
user@mylaptop$ ssh user@server.example.com 'quota'
Disk quotas for user user@server.example.com (uid 6017):
Filesystem blocks  quota  limit  grace  files  quota  limit
grace
/dev/mapper/EBSStore01-user_home01
                   604      0 1048576          172      0   40000
```

New terms and **important words** are shown in bold. Words that you see on the screen, in menus or dialog boxes for example, appear in the text like this: "Once we select **Create Application**, we will be presented with a screen that offers details about our database, how to access the application's gear, cloning our new Git repository and more".

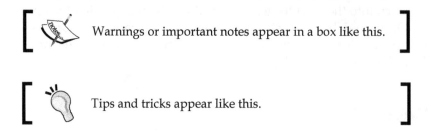

Warnings or important notes appear in a box like this.

Tips and tricks appear like this.

Reader feedback

Feedback from our readers is always welcome. Let us know what you think about this book—what you liked or may have disliked. Reader feedback is important for us to develop titles that you really get the most out of.

To send us general feedback, simply send an e-mail to feedback@packtpub.com, and mention the book title via the subject of your message.

If there is a topic that you have expertise in and you are interested in either writing or contributing to a book, see our author guide on www.packtpub.com/authors.

Customer support

Now that you are the proud owner of a Packt book, we have a number of things to help you to get the most from your purchase.

Downloading the example code

You can download the example code files for all Packt books you have purchased from your account at http://www.packtpub.com. If you purchased this book elsewhere, you can visit http://www.packtpub.com/support and register to have the files e-mailed directly to you.

Errata

Although we have taken every care to ensure the accuracy of our content, mistakes do happen. If you find a mistake in one of our books—maybe a mistake in the text or the code—we would be grateful if you would report this to us. By doing so, you can save other readers from frustration and help us improve subsequent versions of this book. If you find any errata, please report them by visiting http://www.packtpub.com/submit-errata, selecting your book, clicking on the **errata submission form link**, and entering the details of your errata. Once your errata are verified, your submission will be accepted and the errata will be uploaded on our website, or added to any list of existing errata, under the Errata section of that title. Any existing errata can be viewed by selecting your title from http://www.packtpub.com/support.

Piracy

Piracy of copyright material on the Internet is an ongoing problem across all media. At Packt, we take the protection of our copyright and licenses very seriously. If you come across any illegal copies of our works, in any form, on the Internet, please provide us with the location address or website name immediately so that we can pursue a remedy.

Please contact us at copyright@packtpub.com with a link to the suspected pirated material.

We appreciate your help in protecting our authors, and our ability to bring you valuable content.

Questions

You can contact us at questions@packtpub.com if you are having a problem with any aspect of the book, and we will do our best to address it.

1
Understanding the Essentials

This might be an old adage but it most certainly doesn't make it any less true: before we learn to run, we must first learn to walk, and even before that, we must learn to crawl. Effectively, this chapter will progress through a little crawling and then some walking in the world of **Cloud Technologies**, **SSH utility**, **Git Source Control Management** software, and onto **OpenShift**. You'll be running in no time. If you are well versed in the topics leading up to the OpenShift specifics, please feel free to simply skim through the sections offering this background information or skip them altogether as they will most likely be review material. However, if this is new territory to you, please proceed. For those who have some experience in this area, hopefully the following passages will be a helpful refresher.

The Cloud

The mythical creature known as "The Cloud" has become a juggernaut of marketing collateral that often makes those who are technologically inclined want to laugh hysterically or run for the hills. However, it is in fact a paradigm of Information Technology that has taken the market by storm and has no inclination of leaving any time soon. Aside from the marketing hype, this concept of the cloud is truly an evolution of IT that aims to make lives easier for those who use, manage, design, and implement technology. Within the notion of "The Cloud", there are three main **Service Models**, as per the **National Institute of Standards and Technology (NIST)** definition of Cloud Computing (http://csrc.nist.gov/publications/nistpubs/800-145/SP800-145.pdf), or areas of the cloud that are different in their advantages and disadvantages as well as their goals and feature sets. The three service models are:

- Infrastructure as a Service (IaaS)
- Platform as a Service (PaaS)
- Software as a Service (SaaS)

Each of these is listed "as a **Service**" because the cloud is largely about taking traditional components from Information Technology and offering them as a service either to customers or users within an organization in order to provide a more flexible environment. One thing to note here is that these service models are loosely coupled such that we may use them together, but we do not inherently require all the layers in order to create a cloud architecture.

It was mentioned that the cloud has layers. This is mostly an attempt to help us understand how it all fits together, where the distinction between the service models exists, the roles they play, and how each can be applicable to their target user base. We can visualize these different service models as layers built upon one another, not unlike that of a stack. The lower you are in the stack, the more components you, as a user, are responsible for managing, and the higher you are in the stack, the more your service provider is responsible for. The following diagram will show this example, and further explanation will follow in the coming sections in this chapter:

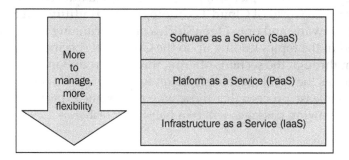

Service models of cloud computing

Infrastructure as a Service (IaaS)

Beginning at the bottom of our stack, we will find the foundation upon which other layers will often be built. This layer is known as **Infrastructure as a Service (IaaS)**, and it has become a part of the natural evolution to traditional virtualization technologies largely deployed in data centers all over the world. Within an IaaS cloud environment, all the aspects of an infrastructure are virtualized into an abstraction structure. With the introduction of this abstraction, we allow for these components to be utilized in a more flexible manner. Often found within IaaS Clouds are virtualized **compute nodes**, which are equivalent to traditional virtual machines but are more dynamic or ephemeral in nature. Storage is considered to be virtualized as well and is deployed in a scaled-out approach, generally offering block storage both as ephemeral resources or as persistent disks. Also common among IaaS environments are virtual networks and virtual firewalls allowing for the separation of resources on the network by creating network security zones.

As a user of IaaS Cloud, there are no ticketing systems for which we have to file requests in order to retrieve the resources that the systems administration or operations team provide. Instead, the service model offers the ability to simply provide what is needed. IaaS offers its power and flexibility at this point where we, as a user, are left to make decisions on criteria such as:

- **Operating System Deployment (OSD)**
- **Service Daemon Configuration (SDC)**
- **Storage Provisioning (SP)**
- **Network Configuration (NC)**
- **Backups**

While these items are criteria that attribute to the flexibility of IaaS, they also incur the overhead of needing a DevOps team or, at a minimum, someone on the staff knowledgeable in the area of DevOps and dedicated to the project at hand. There are a number of open source IaaS solutions that have gained considerable popularity, which will provide great examples and a wealth of documentation for readers who would like to continue on their education in this space. This list is alphabetical and possibly not all-inclusive:

- Apache CloudStack: `https://cloudstack.apache.org/`
- Eucalyptus: `http://www.eucalyptus.com/`
- Nimbus: `http://www.nimbusproject.org/`
- OpenNebula: `http://www.opennebula.org/`
- OpenStack: `http://www.openstack.org/`

DevOps is a new paradigm where the Dev and Ops teams work together in order to solve the need for increased release cycles. The term has been coined by a movement in response to the widening gap between the Dev and Ops teams. It is aimed to solve the problems where a Dev team would write code and hand it over to the Ops team and there was very little coordination between the two. DevOps utilizes the aspects of the cloud, configuration management, and automation tools to satisfy the Dev team's requirement for fast-moving environments, and the Ops team's requirement of a stable and controlled infrastructure.

The common tools in this area are the configuration management software, and readers interested in this area are encouraged to read up on one or many of the following (listed alphabetically):

- Ansible: `http://www.ansibleworks.com/`
- Bcfg2: `https://trac.mcs.anl.gov/projects/bcfg2`
- Chef: `http://www.opscode.com/chef/`
- Puppet: `http://puppetlabs.com/`
- Salt: `http://saltstack.org/`

Platform as a Service (PaaS)

Moving up one layer in our stack example, we find ourselves at **Platform as a Service (PaaS)**. This service model aims to offer some of the flexibility of an IaaS while removing a great deal of the overhead such as the need to maintain the operating system, storage, deployment, provisioning, and configuration management. The offerings in this space will take the abstraction one level higher, and instead of virtualizing every component of the infrastructure that would normally be provisioned as hardware, PaaS effectively offers the pieces of a puzzle, which when put together, provide the platform on which applications can run. In a PaaS environment, the administrators, developers, or deployment managers of web applications can select the components upon which their application will run, such as the service daemon, programming language, web framework, and database. At this point, the end user's decision should focus more on whether the PaaS being reviewed offers features needed by the individual interested in hosting, deploying, or developing a particular application, along with its capacity, scaling, backup, and any other potential concerns.

Now, there are a number of PaaS providers available and anyone looking to select one should indeed spend some time with their favorite search engine to find candidates interested in becoming their provider. The top contenders should also be taken for a test drive before making any hard decisions. However, since this book is about OpenShift, I hope the reader has decided to use OpenShift, and other PaaS providers will not be discussed as such. One thing to note as a tie-in with the stack analogy is how some PaaS architectures are tightly integrated with IaaS using an **Application Programming Interface (API)**. The API can be used as a means of automating tasks within IaaS from the perspective of PaaS, such as launching a new compute node, auto-configuring its storage and services daemons, and adding these new resources to the PaaS environment to increase capacity. Also note that even if PaaS Clouds are not integrated directly to IaaS, they are often deployed on top of IaaS because of the flexible nature of IaaS Clouds.

Software as a Service (SaaS)

Sitting on the top layer of the stack, **Software as a Service (SaaS)** is the cloud evolution of hosted web applications. This layer of abstraction removes the largest amount of control from the user or customer as they take upon the role of simply a user, or possibly as an application administrator, and the entire platform upon which it runs is managed by the service provider as well as all the infrastructure concerns. However, as with all things where there is "give", there must be "take", and in this scenario, the "give" is a loss of control and flexibility in terms of architectural decisions, choice of backend programming languages, frameworks, databases, and any other selections of technology used. The "take" side of this and why this service model gains such widespread adoption is that some organizations, companies, or teams do not have the expertise, the desire to take on the technical aspects of a hosted web application, or might consider such functions as a burden. Common examples of SaaS hosting are **Customer Relations Management (CRM)**, **Enterprise Resource Planning (ERP)**, **Management Information Systems (MIS)**, as well as other essential business-focused software solutions.

SSH

Where did all the clouds go? Why are we talking about SSH all of a sudden? Well, we're talking about SSH because it is an important component of OpenShift as well as other PaaS Clouds. **SSH** is an acronym for **Secure Shell** and it is a network communications protocol that creates encrypted connections for remote command executions, shell sessions, and data transfer. From a user's standpoint, SSH is quite simple to use, but do not let that be an indication of its potential as it is quite powerful. We will briefly discuss some simple SSH commands in context to the OpenShift use cases, but first, we need to understand a couple of things about how SSH works so that we can set up some prerequisites. The first thing on our list of prerequisites is the fact that SSH offers public- or private-key-based authentication, which is extremely common and is also used by OpenShift. The most popular implementation of SSH is arguably **OpenSSH** (http://www.openssh.com/), which is used by OpenShift. OpenSSH can also use other methods for authentication, such as passwords, **Single sign-on mechanisms**, and even **Two-factor authentication**. These alternatives are not covered here as they are not applicable to our coverage of OpenShift.

Once public keys are in place, something that OpenShift's client utilities will set up for us, we can simply run the following command to connect to a remote server in order to run commands in an interactive shell.

> If we are doing this against a server that is not an OpenShift Gear, we will have to verify whether the configurations are in place to allow for passwordless SSH; there are many guides on this online so we won't discuss it here.
>
> Gears will be explained at length in a later section, but it's effectively a GNU/Linux sandbox environment that is resource constrained and secured with SELinux.

```
user@mylaptop$ ssh username@server.example.com
user@server.example.com$
```

If you are using a GNU/Linux distribution or Mac OS X, you will most likely have an SSH client preinstalled; however, if you are a Windows user, you will need to install a third-party SSH client application such as **PuTTY** (http://www.putty.org/).

In the preceding example, the shell prompt, `user@mylaptop$`, is used to signify a shell on the local machine, and once the SSH connection is established, the prompt changes to `user@server.example.com$`, signifying that the shell session that is currently at our fingertips is on a different machine. While shell prompts will vary greatly in the wild because of the flexibility of their configuration, this should serve as a decent placeholder to understand that once we are typing into a shell prompt at `user@server.example.com$`, these commands are happening remotely.

The following diagram shows a simple layout of a client computer (such as a laptop) and a server system, along with a sample user account that resides on the server system, cleverly named user that will offer itself as a high-level overview of the introductory example we previously covered.

 There are actually a lot of steps going on in the background of this diagram that have to do with setting up the encrypted connection, but an in-depth coverage of these is not within the scope of this publication.

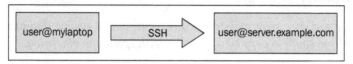

An overview of SSH

Another thing we can do with SSH, other than logging in to a remote shell, is execute single commands remotely and receive their output in the local terminal. The following example will display how to obtain our quota information from an OpenShift Gear using the quota command, without actually entering into an interactive shell session remotely.

OpenShift shell prompts do not actually look like this in real usage; the prompt in the example was modified to maintain consistency with the previous examples. The actual OpenShift prompts and SSH username formatting will be covered in later sections.

```
user@mylaptop$ ssh user@server.example.com 'quota'
Disk quotas for user user@server.example.com (uid 6017):
Filesystem blocks   quota   limit   grace   files   quota   limit
grace
/dev/mapper/EBSStore01-user_home01
                 604      0 1048576            172       0   40000
```

As we can see here, the command was executed remotely and the output was sent back to us providing seamless interaction, almost as though we ran the command locally.

SSH is often just used outside interactive shells and remote-command execution. Many utilities in traditional Unix and Unix-like operating systems use or have the option to use SSH as their data transport in order to provide secure transmission of whatever data they need to move between two hosts. Common utilities in this category are rsync, scp, mercurial (hg), and git, which leads us into the next section based on git.

Git

Once upon a time, developers would maintain complex directory structures of source code that would live on a central server. Members of the development team would mount the directory over a shared file system or develop collectively on the same server, both of which posed a laundry list of problems. There is a classification of utility known as **Version Control Systems (VCSs)**, which solve these issues. VCSs create the ability to maintain a manifest of differentials between "commits" or "versions" of a code base and much more. The VCS of choice for code management and deployment with OpenShift is named **Git**. The following is an excerpt from the Git website (`http://git-scm.com/`):

> *"Git is a free and open source distributed version control system designed to handle everything from small to very large projects with speed and efficiency.*
>
> *Git is easy to learn and has a tiny footprint with lightning fast performance. It outclasses SCM tools like Subversion, CVS, Perforce, and ClearCase with features like cheap local branching, convenient staging areas, and multiple workflows".*

Before we go too deep into the details of Git, there needs to be some discussion about a few Git concepts that are essential to understanding how Git functions and why it is so powerful for developers. The first of which is the notion of a **branch**. In Git, there is the source-code repository that has been initialized to be tracked, and within that repository, there can be many branches. A branch is effectively a sub-repository snapshot that maintains its own change logs, snapshots, metadata, and so on. A Git branch is not a unique concept as other version control systems share this feature, but many who have never experienced it might find it difficult to follow at first, so hopefully the following diagram will help to clarify:

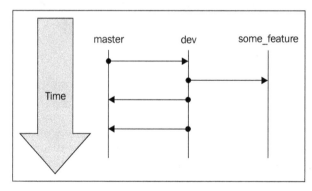

Overview of the Git branch

In the preceding diagram, there are three lines, each representing a branch. A focal point to make note of is what is known as the **master** branch, which is created by default when you create and initialize a Git repository. It stands to note that at the time a branch is created, it is a point-in-time snapshot of the code base from where the branch originates, and each branch can receive code commits independently from one another. Within the diagram, in this hypothetical Git repository, there are two other branches. One is called `dev` and another is called `some_feature`, both of which are meant to show that this is all the same code base but has deviations during the development timeline. The arrows moving between the branches introduce another concept from Git called a **merge**. In Git, when you merge from one branch to another, you are applying the change set or differential from another branch upon the current one. Git has a number of clever methods for accomplishing this task, but it should be mentioned that there is a possibility of a conflict that would have to be resolved before the merge operation can be completed. There are methods for mitigating the risk of merge conflicts, which will be discussed later in this section. The manner in which developers perform their branch-and-merge process is up to their respective development team. There are many approaches to branch/merge development cycles, each with advantages and disadvantages, and discussions of these exist far and wide on the Internet. It is advisable to spend some time researching to find the one that best fits a project's development style.

This has been a very rapid discussion of Git concepts, and we have only scraped the surface of its power and distributed nature. It would be advisable to spend some time with the Git project's documentation (http://git-scm.com/doc) for users who are interested in the breadth of capability that Git offers.

Hopefully, there is enough background information covered up to this point in order to start working with Git, so we will first want to set up a couple of global parameters for good measure.

While it was not covered here, it is assumed that Git is installed on the user's system. For GNU/Linux users of debian-based distributions, this can be done with `apt-get install git` as the root (or the `git-all` package to pull in all subpackages) or from a Fedora- or Red Hat-based system, it can be accomplished using `yum install git` as the root. Other Linux distributions are likely to have the installable package name of `git` in their respective repositories. For users of Mac OS X or Windows, please visit Git's download site (http://git-scm.com/downloads) in order to obtain your installation medium.

When using Git for the first time, the first order of business is to set a few global Git settings such as developer identity, editor of choice, and diff tool (for merges). Run the following commands as the system user (that is, as a non-root user), which will be used for development, replacing the name and e-mail address with your own:

```
$ git config --global user.name "John Smith"
$ git config --global user.email johnsmith@example.com
```

Next up on the list will be to configure the editor of choice. Most developers like to use either `vim` or `emacs`, but these are certainly not the only editors in town, so use what fits best. We can configure the editor as follows:

```
$ git config --global core.editor vim
```

After these are in place, it would also be wise to configure a **merge tool**, which is used to assist when handling the merge conflicts. On my system, which is Fedora 19, at the time of writing, the command `git mergetool -tool-help` lists the following as valid entries as a merge tool: `araxis`, `bc3`, `codecompare`, `diffuse`, `ecmerge`, `emerge`, `gvimdiff`, `kdiff3`, `meld`, `opendiff`, `p4merge`, `tkdiff`, `tortoisemerge`, `vimdiff`, and `xxdiff`. These tools are simple examples of merge utilities that can be used, and we should select one we feel comfortable with, or accept the defaults for your system if this is uncharted territory. For those using a GNU/Linux distribution as their development platform of choice, and who enjoy graphical environments, `meld` and `kdiff3` have both received a lot of positive feedback and would likely be a decent place to start. As a `vim` user, `vimdiff` is the merge tool of choice and we'll configure it as follows:

```
$ git config --global merge.tool vimdiff
```

There are also a number of other configurable Git variables, which may be found using either the Git documentation found on their website or via the `git-config` main page.

Moving on, for the sake of the example, let's assume that there is an application we are going to write named `my_app`. For simplicity, it will just be a simple "Hello World" example in Ruby, but it will be enough to cover the basic usage commands. First, we need a directory that we will turn into a Git repository using the following commands:

```
$ mkdir my_app
$ cd my_app
$ git init
Initialized empty Git repository in ~/myapp/.git/
```

That's it. That's the magic; we did it! See how easy that was? It is truly amazing how powerful Git is, considering how simple it is to use. Next up, we need to create a file named app.rb with the following contents:

```
#!/usr/bin/env ruby

puts "Hello world!"
```

> **Downloading the example code**
>
> You can download the example code files for all Packt books you have purchased from your account at http://www.packtpub.com. If you purchased this book elsewhere, you can visit http://www.packtpub.com/support and register to have the files e-mailed directly to you.

> The #!/usr/bin/env ruby line is what is called a **shebang,** and it defines the environment in which the file should be executed. This is a common Unix-ism and will have no effect on the Windows environments.

Since we have a file and some contents, we'll now need to add it to git in order to be tracked by Git using the following command:

```
$ git add app.rb
```

Then to check the status of our Git repository, run the following command and you should get a similar output:

```
$ git status
# On branch master
#
# Initial commit
#
# Changes to be committed:
#   (use "git rm --cached <file>..." to unstage)
#
#   new file:    app.rb
#
```

The portion of these lines of commands that is of interest is the `Changes to be committed` part. This means we've added changes to a "staging" status and it is ready to be committed to the Git log. Also, we can add a `commit` message to provide some context to what the contents of this commit are. We will commit and then check the Git log; remember, Git maintains a log of all the code that is committed to the repository. Commit the code and view the Git logs with the following commands:

```
$ git commit -m "Initial commit of app.rb, Hello World example"
[master (root-commit) 77839fd] Initial commit of app.rb, Hello World
example
1 file changed, 3 insertions(+)
create mode 100644 app.rb

$ git log
commit 77839fdef6f17012797e93f05516d342570d31d6
Author: Adam Miller <maxamillion@fedoraproject.org>
Date:   Wed Jan 9 23:21:04 2013 -0600
Initial commit of app.rb, Hello World example
```

One thing to note here is that if you were to run the command, `git show`, it will show you the latest entry in the Git log, including the changes committed as follows. We will see the line start with two paths that don't really exist, `a/app.rb` and `b/app.rb`, these are effectively placeholders that show the differential between what `app.rb` used to be and what it is now within this Git branch:

```
$ git show
commit 77839fdef6f17012797e93f05516d342570d31d6
Author: Adam Miller <maxamillion@fedoraproject.org>
Date:   Wed Jan 9 23:21:04 2013 -0600


    Initial commit of app.rb, Hello World example


diff --git a/app.rb b/app.rb
new file mode 100644
index 0000000..2966711
--- /dev/null
+++ b/app.rb
@@ -0,0 +1,3 @@
+#!/usr/bin/env ruby
+
+puts "Hello world!"
```

In the preceding output, there is a **commit** ID, which is a unique identifier for this commit, followed by the **Author** and **Date** stamp for the commit.

 A quick side mention that should be considered is that date stamps are not always chronologically ordered as we might think they should be, and this can happen in a number of ways, but most commonly, are going to be time zones of commits in a distributed development model or merges intermingling commits.

After the **commit** ID, the **Author**, and the **Date** stamp, is the commit message and the **diff**. For those familiar with the `diff` and `patch` tools, they will feel right at home with this output formatting and its meanings. If this is new territory, fret not as the output is relatively straightforward: the lines with a + character prepended are additions to the file, lines with a - character prepended are removals from the file, lines without any prepended characters are not modified, and lines with the @@ characters are offsets in the file.

If the Git repository we were working with had not been initialized on our local machine, but instead had been cloned from a remote repository, which is what happens when you use OpenShift, there would be one more command needed to propagate this commit to the remote server: `git push`. Do you remember we have mentioned before that Git is distributed, and therefore, the commit we made previously was only to our local repository? By performing a `git push`, we are "pushing" those changes out to a remote location. The default remote location in Git nomenclature is known as `origin`, but we need not supply that information to the command because by default it is assumed.

 Note that the following output is from an OpenShift Git repository and will contain some output that might not be very meaningful, but don't worry as this will be covered at length in the later sections.

```
$ git push
Counting objects: 4, done.
Delta compression using up to 4 threads.
Compressing objects: 100% (2/2), done.
Writing objects: 100% (3/3), 290 bytes, done.
Total 3 (delta 1), reused 0 (delta 0)
remote: restart_on_add=false
remote: Waiting for stop to finish
remote: Done
```

```
remote: restart_on_add=false

remote: ~/git/sinatra.git ~/git/sinatra.git

remote: ~/git/sinatra.git

remote: Running .openshift/action_hooks/pre_build

remote: Running .openshift/action_hooks/build

remote: Running .openshift/action_hooks/deploy

remote: hot_deploy_added=false

remote: Done

remote: Running .openshift/action_hooks/post_deploy

To ssh://891a6370bd884b348305552b1c9485e7@sinatra-admiller.rhcloud.com/~/
git/sinatra.git/

  bab6f7c..e703aa8  master -> master
```

OpenShift – a bird's-eye view

In this section we will discuss OpenShift at a very high level, showing certain components of the backend, explaining a little about how everything fits together and how it works, without getting too much in depth with each. That level of granularity will be explored in later sections and might not be applicable to everyone's interests.

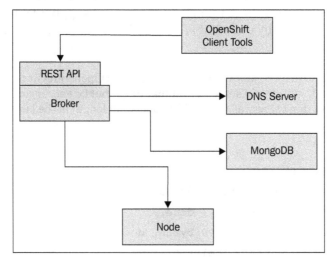

OpenShift—a bird's-eye view

Following the preceding diagram, we will walk through the path where traffic will flow, starting with the perspective of a user utilizing the OpenShift Client Tools. From there, we will proceed by stepping through the components so that we can get a basic feel of the way the platform works before diving deeper into the individual levels. Both the DNS server and the MongoDB system will not receive much focus at this time as DNS and database servers are conceptually extremely widespread technologies and this is meant to be a high-level discussion; they will, however, receive focus in later sections. OpenShift is written in the Ruby programming language (`http://www.ruby-lang.org`) using the very popular Ruby on Rails (`http://rubyonrails.org/`) web framework. This will be noteworthy for any reader who may be interested in joining the OpenShift Origin upstream development community.

> Ruby is an open source, multi-platform, object-oriented programming language that has gained considerable popularity in recent years, especially in the realm of web development in large, thanks to the Ruby on Rails web framework, which is also open source. More information on each of these, respectively, can be found at `http://www.ruby-lang.org/en/http://rubyonrails.org/`.

Client tools

The layer where OpenShift users will spend most of their time developing or hosting their web application is the client tools. The client tools will communicate with the server known as a **broker**, which we will cover shortly. Within the category of client tools, there are a number of options: first is the command-line interface that is distributed as a RubyGem. The Gem itself is distributed on `https://rubygems.org/gems/rhc`, and more information about it and its code base can be found on GitHub (`https://github.com/openshift/rhc/`).

> A RubyGem is a package management format that is the standard for distributing and consuming software, and software libraries written in the Ruby programming language. These packages are often repackaged into GNU/Linux distribution's native package format such as `rpm` or `deb` so that it can be easily deployed and installed. For more information about RubyGems, visit `https://rubygems.org/`.

Aside from the RubyGem version of the command-line client tools, there are also various **Integrated Development Environments (IDEs)** that offer integration as well as the Web Console, all of which allow for the developer to utilize the OpenShift platform. At the time of this writing, the Red Hat JBoss Developer Studio, which is an IDE from Red Hat based on Eclipse (`https://devstudio.jboss.com`), an Eclipse plugin, and the Zend Studio IDEs, offer OpenShift client-integration plugins. However, it should be noted that no matter the utility, all end user tools utilize the **Representational State Transfer Application Programming Interface (REST API)** on the backend. This will be covered in more detail later.

Broker

Interaction with OpenShift happens through the broker. This component of OpenShift can be thought of as the facilitator, as it handles REST API calls and translates them into actions. These actions can be DNS updates, user authentication, or an application action such as creation, deletion, or other state changes. When these actions are sent to the broker, it will make its decisions and utilize a message-passing mechanism to instruct other components within OpenShift to carry out a task. Depending on the task required, the broker will send a message such as the following to a supporting system:

- Name server record updates
- Application state transition
- User authentication
- Node tasks: performing actions against a user's application environment

Node

When an OpenShift user creates an application, they do so within a container that has been titled as **Gear**, and multiple OpenShift gears will live on a single **Node**. Multiple nodes can exist in an OpenShift environment, but the important point to be observed here, which makes the OpenShift PaaS unique, is that it's multitenant at the operating system level or at the platform layer, which offers high density. These nodes are the work horses. This is where the applications run, the databases run, the Git repositories live, as well as what is known as a **Cartridge** will execute (more on cartridges later), and the location that we will land at when we SSH into our application or Gear.

Summary

This has been a whirlwind take on all things in cloud computing and most notably that of Platform as a Service. In this chapter, we have also covered some background utilities such as SSH and Git that are essential for using OpenShift, and we even took a high-level look into the OpenShift architecture in order to see how all the components fit together. Next up, we will move on to actually using OpenShift by utilizing the hosted free OpenShift Online service, as we explore all the ways we are able to deploy our applications into "The Cloud" using OpenShift.

2
Using OpenShift

In *Chapter 1, Understanding the Essentials*, we discussed a number of technologies, including coverage of the Cloud and its service model paradigms, SSH, and Git, and a very high-level overview of the OpenShift Architecture in order to gain perspective on how all the components combine to deliver a platform as a service. Now, we are about to begin utilizing this platform for our development or web application hosting needs.

The following are the three common ways in which we can utilize OpenShift as a user:

- Command-line utilities
- Web Console
- IDE integration

Each of these utilize the OpenShift REST API at the backend; therefore, as a user, we could potentially orchestrate OpenShift using the API with such common command-line utilities as `curl` to write scripts for automation. We could also use the API to write our own custom user interface, if we had the desire. In the following sections, we will explore using each of the currently supported user experiences, all of which can be intermixed as they communicate with the backend in a uniform fashion using the REST API previously mentioned.

Getting started using OpenShift

As discussed previously, we will be using the OpenShift Online free hosted service for example portions. OpenShift Online has the lowest barrier of entry from a user's perspective because we will not have to deploy our own OpenShift PaaS before being able to utilize it. Since we will be using the OpenShift Online service, the very first step is going to be to visit their website and sign up for a free account via `https://openshift.redhat.com/app/account/new`.

New account form

Once this step is complete, we will find an e-mail in our inbox that was provided during sign up, with a subject line similar to **Confirm your Red Hat OpenShift account**; inside that e-mail will be a URL that needs to be followed to complete the setup and verification step. Now that we've successfully completed the sign up phase, let's move on to exploring the different ways in which we can use and interact with OpenShift.

Command-line utilities

Due to the advancements in modern computing and the advent of mobile devices such as tablets, smart phones, and many other devices, we are often accustomed to **Graphical User Interface (GUI)** over **Command-Line Interface (CLI)** for most of our computing needs. This trend is heavier in the realm of web applications because of the rich visual experiences that can be delivered using next generation web technologies. However, those of us who are in the development and system administration circles of the world are no strangers to the CLI, and we know that it is often the most powerful way to accomplish an array of tasks pertaining to development and administration. Much of this is a credit to powerful shell environments that have their roots in traditional UNIX environments; popular examples of these are bash and zsh. Also, in more recent years, PowerShell for the Microsoft Windows platform has aimed to provide some relatively similar CLI power.

> The shell, as it is referenced here, is that of a UNIX shell, which is a command interpreter that supports such features as variables, functions, pipes, I/O redirection, variable substitution, flow control, conditionals, the ability to be scripted, and more. There is also a POSIX standard for a shell that defines a standard set of features and behaviors that must be complied with, allowing for portability of complex scripts.

With this inherent power at the fingertips of the person who wields the command line, the development team of the OpenShift PaaS has written a command-line utility, much in the spirit of offering powerful utilities to its users and developers. Before we get too deep into the details, let's quickly look at what a normal application creation and deployment requires in OpenShift using the following command:

```
$ rhc app create myawesomewebapp ruby-1.9
$ cd myawesomewebapp


(Write, create, and implement code changes)


$ git commit -a -m "wrote awesome code"
$ git push
```

It will be discussed at length shortly, but for a quick rundown, the `rhc app create myawesomewebapp ruby-1.9` command creates an application, which runs on OpenShift using `ruby-1.9` as the programming platform. Behind the scenes, it's provisioning space, resources, and configuring services for us. It also creates a `git` repository that is then cloned locally—in our example named `myawesomewebapp`—and in order to access this, we need to change directories into the `git` repository. That is precisely what the next command `cd myawesomewebapp` does. Finally, the `git` commands should look familiar to the commands in *Chapter 1, Understanding the Essentials*.

And you're live, running your web application in the cloud. While this is an extremely high-level overview and there are some prerequisites necessary, normal use of OpenShift is that easy. In the following section, we will discuss at length all the steps necessary to launch a live application in OpenShift Online using the `rhc` command-line utility and `git`.

This command-line utility, `rhc`, is written in the Ruby programming language and is distributed as a RubyGem (`https://rubygems.org/`). This is the recommended method of installation for Ruby modules, libraries, and utilities due to the platform-independent nature of Ruby and the ease of distribution of gems.

The `rhc` command-line utility is also available using the native package management for both Fedora and Red Hat Enterprise Linux (via the EPEL repository, available at `https://fedoraproject.org/wiki/EPEL`) by running the `yum install rubygem-rhc` command.

Another noteworthy proponent of RubyGems is that they can be installed to a user's home directory within their local machine's operating system, allowing them to be utilized even in environments where systems are centrally managed by an IT department. RubyGems are also installed using the gem package manager for users of GNU/Linux package managers, such as `yum`, `apt-get`, and `pacman` or Mac OS X's community homebrew (`brew`) package manager, which will be familiar with the concept. For those unfamiliar with these concepts, a package manager will track a software named "package" and its dependencies, handle installation, updates, as well as removal. We will take a short moment to tangent into the topic of RubyGems before moving on to the command-line utility for OpenShift to ensure that we don't leave out any background information.

The following sections will assume that we have Ruby and RubyGems installed. If that is not the case, now would be the time to follow the installation instructions for both of these at the following URLs respectively:

`http://www.ruby-lang.org/en/downloads/` and `https://rubygems.org/pages/download`

These can also be installed using the local package manager for your GNU or Linux distribution of choice. Ruby comes installed by default on Mac OS X; as of now the latest version available at this time is Mountain Lion (10.8).

The following command will install the gem of the OpenShift client tools called `rhc`, which is available at `https://rubygems.org/gems/rhc`; also, note that specific versions are likely to vary as development continues on gems:

```
$ gem install rhc

Fetching: rhc-1.13.6.gem (100%)

Fetching: httpclient-2.3.2.gem (100%) =====================================
====================
If this is your first time installing the RHC tools, please run 'rhc
setup'

==========================================================
Successfully installed httpclient-2.3.2

Successfully installed rhc-1.13.6

2 gems installed

Installing ri documentation for httpclient-2.3.2...

Installing ri documentation for rhc-1.13.6...

Installing RDoc documentation for httpclient-2.3.2...

Installing RDoc documentation for rhc-1.13.6...
```

There are a couple of things to note from the preceding output. If we previously did not have the RubyGems system or any preexisting gems installed, we would likely see considerably more output, as more dependencies would be downloaded and installed. If this is the case, don't be alarmed, as this is normal. This also helps to not overload the example with unnecessary output. If we were to take a moment to look at the listing of the currently installed gems, we could run the following command to get a reporting (some lines are omitted for brevity):

```
$ gem list -local

activesupport (3.2.9)
```

```
addressable (2.3.2)
archive-tar-minitar (0.5.2)
aws-sdk (1.6.5)
bigdecimal (1.1.0)
builder (3.1.4)
bundler (1.1.4)
.

... (omitted output) ....

.
rhc (1.13.6, 1.12.4, 1.3.8, 1.2.7, 1.1.11)
rspec (1.3.2)
ruby-lint (0.0.2)
... (omitted output) ....
```

The main point to note from the preceding output is that the `rhc` gem has multiple versions listed in the parenthesis next to its gem name. This is to signify that there are multiple versions installed. In the event it were a software library instead of a command-line utility, we may want to maintain multiple versions installed in parallel. Another neat feature is that gems can signify a dependency upon specific versions of the libraries or utilities they require; this parallel install flexibility allows different gems to not be restricted to requiring the same versions of the things they depend upon from the RubyGems repository. For more information on the capabilities of the gem utility, run the `gem help` command.

Now that we are a little more familiar with what RubyGems are and the capabilities of the gem utility, we can move on to using our OpenShift client utility, which we installed in a previous example, called `rhc`. As noted in the output of the `gem install rhc` command, we were presented with the **If this is your first time installing the RHC tools, please run 'rhc setup'** message, and we will assume that is in fact the case and will follow along with that.

At the time of writing, the latest released version of `rhc` was `1.13.6` and that is what will be used for the duration of the text—the exact output from the utility or some interactions are subject to change in later versions. In the event of inconsistencies, always refer to the upstream project's documentation at `https://www.openshift.com/get-started/`.

```
$ rhc setup
OpenShift Client Tools (RHC) Setup Wizard
```

This wizard will help you upload your SSH keys, set your application namespace, and check that other programs like Git are properly installed.

Login to openshift.redhat.com: username@example.com

Password: ************

Saving configuration to /home/adam/.openshift/express.conf ... done

No SSH keys were found. We will generate a pair of keys for you.

    Created: /home/adam/.ssh/id_rsa.pub

Your public SSH key must be uploaded to the OpenShift server to access code. Upload now? (yes|no) yes

Since you do not have any keys associated with your OpenShift account, your new key will be uploaded as the 'default' key.

    Type: ssh-rsa

    Fingerprint: 90:31:b1:25:f5:0e:c0:b3:fb:7e:5e:b8:7b:9b:d7:47

Uploading key 'default' from /home/adam/.ssh/id_rsa.pub ... done

Checking for git ... needs to be installed

Automated installation of client tools is not supported for your platform. You will need to manually install git for full OpenShift functionality.

Checking common problems . done

Checking your namespace ... none

Your namespace is unique to your account and is the suffix of the public URLs we assign to your applications. You may configure your namespace here or leave it blank and use 'rhc domain create' to create a namespace later. You will not be able to create applications without first creating a namespace.

```
Please enter a namespace (letters and numbers only) |<none>|: packtbook
Your domain name 'packtbook' has been successfully created

Checking for applications ... none

Run 'rhc app create' to create your first application.

.

... Omitted for brevity...

.


    You are using 0 of 3 total gears
    The following gear sizes are available to you: small

Your client tools are now configured.
```

In the preceding output, we accomplished a number of things; first we allowed the rhc tool to create SSH keys on our behalf and upload them to the OpenShift service. We then were informed that we are lacking an installation of the git utility (this command was run in a base installation of Fedora 19 for example purposes); this is something that can be automatically installed on our behalf for some systems, but not all. I've left this output in the example to show that the utility will install this for us if possible, or at least let us know that git is an essential part of our OpenShift experience, as noted in *Chapter 1, Understanding the Essentials*. Next on the list of things our setup accomplishes for us is that it creates the domain space in which our OpenShift applications will live. When using the OpenShift Online service, this will act as your subdomain of the rhcloud.com web domain space, and all our web applications will be assigned a name in the following format:

```
<application_name>-<domain_name>.rhcloud.com
```

This format is the way in which each user's application may obtain a global DNS entry and still remain unique. In addition to this setup step, we should take a moment to note that OpenShift Online does offer a DNS alias functionality so that we can use our own domain names, if we so choose. The final step from the rhc setup output is showing us the number of application gears we are currently consuming. We covered this in *Chapter 1, Understanding the Essentials*, but I will quickly recap; effectively, a Gear is a resource abstraction that can contain a single "application," which in most cases is equivalent to an application framework or language runtime Cartridge (cartridge being the building blocks that we combine to create the platform upon which we write or run our application). Currently, it is also able to contain one or many add-on cartridges, such as a database, jenkins, or database administrative frontend.

The portion of the output that is omitted in the previous example lists the currently available cartridge types that provide runtimes, databases, and frameworks we may select from, to either develop or deploy on top. This output will be useful shortly, so it was left out to keep the verbosity to a minimum.

Now that we have set up our command-line utilities and defined a domain for our applications to live within, let's explore a little bit of what we can do and see with the command-line utilities. First, let's actually create an application so that we can perform a little bit of development. Note that the development demonstration here will only show a simple example using Ruby 1.9 and the Sinatra web framework (http://www.sinatrarb.com/), but OpenShift supports far more than just this language runtime for application development. In order to obtain a complete list of the application runtimes and frameworks available, run the following command and observe its output. Take into account that this list is subject to change as ongoing development increases the options available to us as users:

```
$ rhc cartridge list
jbossas-7              JBoss Application Server 7                    web
jbosseap-6 (*)         JBoss Enterprise Application Platform 6.1.0 web
jenkins-1              Jenkins Server                                web
nodejs-0.6             Node.js 0.6                                   web
perl-5.10              Perl 5.10                                     web
php-5.3                PHP 5.3                                       web
python-2.6             Python 2.6                                    web
python-2.7             Python 2.7                                    web
python-3.3             Python 3.3                                    web
ruby-1.8               Ruby 1.8                                      web
ruby-1.9               Ruby 1.9                                      web
jbossews-1.0           Tomcat 6 (JBoss EWS 1.0)                      web
jbossews-2.0           Tomcat 7 (JBoss EWS 2.0)                      web
zend-5.6               Zend Server 5.6                               web
diy-0.1                Do-It-Yourself 0.1                            web
10gen-mms-agent-0.1 10gen Mongo Monitoring Service Agent          addon
cron-1.4               Cron 1.4                                      addon
jenkins-client-1       Jenkins Client                               addon
mongodb-2.2            MongoDB NoSQL Database 2.2                    addon
mysql-5.1              MySQL Database 5.1                            addon
```

metrics-0.1	OpenShift Metrics 0.1	addon
haproxy-1.4	OpenShift Web Balancer	addon
phpmyadmin-3	phpMyAdmin 3.4	addon
postgresql-8.4	PostgreSQL Database 8.4	addon
postgresql-9.2	PostgreSQL Database 9.2	addon
rockmongo-1.1	RockMongo 1.1	addon
switchyard-0	SwitchYard 0.8.0	addon

Note: Web cartridges can only be added to new applications.

(*) denotes a cartridge with additional usage costs.

There are two things that can be taken away from the preceding output. The first is that there are designations between a web cartridge and an addon cartridge. A web cartridge is going to be either a language runtime or a web framework. You may not combine multiple web frameworks within a single gear, but may combine a single web cartridge and one or many add-on cartridges, provided they are compatible (that is, you wouldn't combine phpmyadmin with postgresql-8.4 as phpmyadmin is made for use with the MySQL database). The second take away is that, in some instances, such as the Ruby programming language cartridge in the preceding output, it is possible that there are more than single versions of a cartridge currently supported, which offers us flexibility in our choices as the end user. This, however, adds some overhead to our rhc commands in order to specify the version. One nice thing to combat this is that, as of the rhc version 1.13.6, and likely in all newer versions, the ability to "short hand" cartridge names is now supported, as we will see shortly.

At this point, it is time to create an application using our `rhc` command-line utilities. We can name our application almost anything we would like, but the name must be alphanumeric and cannot contain a - character. For this example, we will be using the application named as `sinatra` since that is the framework we will be using:

```
$ rhc app create sinatra ruby-1.9
Application Options

------------------

  Namespace:  packtbook
  Cartridges: ruby-1.9
  Gear Size:  default
  Scaling:    no


Creating application 'sinatra' ... done


Waiting for your DNS name to be available ... done


Downloading the application Git repository ...
Cloning into 'sinatra'...


Your application code is now in 'sinatra'


sinatra @ http://sinatra-packtbook.rhcloud.com/ (uuid:
be1556f7c367494899b7a3fac08b746e) ----------------------------------------
----------------------------------------- --------

  Created: 10:38 PM   Gears:  1 (defaults to small)
  Git URL: ssh://be1556f7c367494899b7a3fac08b746e@sinatra-packtbook.
rhcloud.com/~/git/sinat ra.git/
  SSH:      be1556f7c367494899b7a3fac08b746e@sinatra-packtbook.rhcloud.com


  ruby-1.9 (Ruby 1.9)
  ------------------
  Gears: 1 small


RESULT:
Application sinatra was created.
```

Upon completion of this command being run, a few things have occurred. First, we have provisioned a gear on the OpenShift Online service by running the `ruby-1.9` cartridge. Next, a DNS entry is created and propagated so that our web application is live and available to us, as well as the world, as soon as its creation is completed. Finally, we will have a local `git` repository within our current working directory with the same name as our application name; in this case it is `sinatra`. As mentioned, our DNS name has been propagated. So, in this example, the application name is `sinatra`, and my previously chosen domain or namespace was `packtbook`. I can then navigate to `http://sinatra-packtbook.rhcloud.com/` and be presented with the **Welcome to OpenShift** starter page, as shown in the following screenshot:

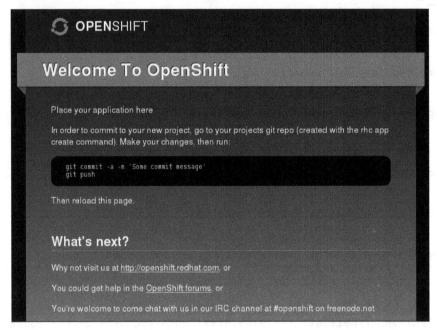

Welcome to OpenShift

Here we see some simple welcome notes and a bit of guidance on what steps must be followed as an OpenShift user. Before going too far, let's look at what OpenShift created for us. In this example, we have the `git` repository named `Sinatra`, and as mentioned before, this is not an ordinary directory; it is in fact a cloned `git` repository whose origin lives on the gear created with the `rhc` client tools. Now let's change directories into our application's cloned `git` repository and take a look at everything that has been laid out for us using the following command:

```
~]$ cd sinatra/

sinatra]$ ls
config.ru  public  README  tmp
```

Here we can see that our `git` repository is not empty but is prepopulated based on the cartridge we selected. So, if your choice of language cartridge was not `ruby-1.9`, your predefined layout could potentially be different. The most important file in this directory is going to be the README file, as it discusses deployment characteristics specific to not only the language cartridge of choice, but also to OpenShift itself. The following is an excerpt from the README file located in this example just to give an idea of some of the information that can be found here:

```
Repo layout
===========
tmp/ - Temporary storage
public/ - Content (images, css, etc. available to the public)
config.ru - This file is used by Rack-based servers to start the
application.
.openshift/action_hooks/pre_build - Script that gets run every git
push before the build
.openshift/action_hooks/build - Script that gets run every git push as
part of the build process (on the CI system if available)
.openshift/action_hooks/deploy - Script that gets run every git push
after build but before the app is restarted
.openshift/action_hooks/post_deploy - Script that gets run every git
push after the app is restarted
.

... Omitted for brevity...
.
```

Something interesting in the output are the `git` hooks; these are scripts that are run at different points during the deployment of your application and can be used for an array of functionality; however, most often, this provides a tie in for **Continuous Integration (CI)**. Also found in this README file is information on how to access gear resources, such as database hostname, port, username, and password all through environment variables so that these need not be stored within your source code. Since we are using the Ruby programming language for this example, the README file also discusses using `Gemfile` along with the RubyGem `bundler` utility (`http://gembundler.com/`). It does so in order to automatically satisfy dependencies and allow users to lock specific versions of dependencies in place with `Gemfile.lock`.

 What is `Gemfile.lock`? `Gemfile.lock` is effectively a manifest built from `Gemfile` that allows you to define a specific "locked" version of all the dependencies of your application.

If you were to select a different language for your development purposes, the contents of this README file would contain specific information for your platform of choice, and I certainly recommend you to familiarize yourself with its contents. Now that we're all familiar with the README file and its inherent power as an information source, let's move on to deploying our demonstration application. First thing we will need is to create our Gemfile file in order to make sure we have the dependencies needed for our example application. We do this using the following code:

```
Edit File: ~/sinatra/Gemfile

source 'http://mirror1.ops.rhcloud.com/mirror/ruby/'
gem 'rack'
gem 'sinatra'
```

We should notice here that our source entry is an OpenShift rhcloud domain entry whose information was provided from the README file. It is also the OpenShift local mirror for rubygems.org so that deployments can occur at a more rapid pace when resolving dependencies. Now that it is in place, the next thing on the agenda is our config.ru file, most likely those familiar with Ruby web development will be familiar with this file, but those who come from other fields just need to know that this is a file used with **rack-based** (http://rack.github.io/) applications. The built in config.ru in our git repo contains code for the production of the OpenShift welcome page but we no longer want that, so we will be effectively deleting and replacing its contents with the following code:

```
Edit File: ~/sinatra/config.ru

require 'rubygems'
require 'bundler'
Bundler.require

require './app.rb'
run Sinatra::Application
```

A short note about what we're doing with config.ru, but first we need to unearth some mystery about Sinatra. Sinatra is a web framework dependent on rack, which is a web server interface allowing for a modular and portable method of developing on the web in Ruby. We use config.ru to tell rack what framework or frameworks, or "middleware", we want to use, and in this case that is Sinatra.

With this in place, we have laid the ground work to run our Sinatra application, which we will call app.rb as noted on the sixth line of our config.ru file. The following is an example of a Sinatra web application and is intentionally left brief so we don't tangent too far into, "How to write Sinatra web applications?" but instead focus on its deployment upon OpenShift. For more information on Sinatra, feel free to visit their upstream project's documentation at http://www.sinatrarb.com/documentation:

```
Edit File: ~/sinatra/app.rb

get '/' do
  "<h1> Awesome! I'm running on OpenShift! </h1>"
end
```

We're all set; next up is just a little bit of git, which we should remember from *Chapter 1, Understanding the Essentials*. We will run git add so that git is tracking our files, then git commit to commit to our local git repository, and then git push to origin. The code to do this is as follows:

```
sinatra]$ git add app.rb config.ru Gemfile

sinatra]$ git commit -m "First commit to OpenShift"
# On branch master
# Your branch is ahead of 'origin/master' by 1 commit.
#   (use "git push" to publish your local commits)
#
nothing to commit, working directory clean

sinatra]$ git push
Counting objects: 7, done.
Compressing objects: 100% (5/5), done.
Writing objects: 100% (5/5), 675 bytes, done.
Total 5 (delta 0), reused 0 (delta 0)
remote: restart_on_add=false
remote: Waiting for stop to finish
remote: Waiting for stop to finish
remote: Waiting for stop to finish
remote: Waiting for stop to finish
remote: Done
remote: restart_on_add=false
remote: Running .openshift/action_hooks/pre_build
remote: Bundling RubyGems based on Gemfile/Gemfile.lock to repo/
vendor/bundle with 'bundle install --deployment'
remote: The --deployment flag requires a Gemfile.lock. Please make
sure you have checked your Gemfile.lock into version control before
deploying.
```

```
remote: Running .openshift/action_hooks/build
remote: Running .openshift/action_hooks/deploy
remote: hot_deploy_added=false
remote: Done
remote: Running .openshift/action_hooks/post_deploy
To ssh://be1556f7c367494899b7a3fac08b746e@sinatra-packtbook.rhcloud.
com/~/git/sinatra.git/
   18de7cf..27fe9d3  master -> master
```

And we're done! We have officially deployed a web application to OpenShift. If you have followed along and visited your application's URL, you should see the following screenshot in your web browser:

A running Ruby application

Now before we switch gears and explore one of the other methods of interacting with OpenShift, we should spend a few moments looking at some commands, mentioned in the following table, that are useful during development:

rhc command	Uses and examples
rhc cartridge list	This will list out all the available cartridges to select from, including the addon cartridges that provide extended functionality.
rhc domain show	This will display information about your application domain namespace, including the information to interface with the gear directly through ssh, as well as connection information about database addon cartridges.
rhc app show	This will show similar information to what rhc domain show does but will only display it for a specific application and not for all applications within the domain namespace.
rhc port-forward	This will allow you to forward a remote port from your application gear to your local workstation.
rhc tail	This command will tail log files from your gear over an ssh tunnel. This is similar to SSHing into your gear and using the tail utility with the -f flag on log files.

rhc command	Uses and examples
`rhc snapshot`	This command will click a snapshot of the current state of our application and save it locally to create a point in time, backing up or restoring from a previous snapshot.
`rhc ssh`	This command will allow you to SSH into your application by name without needing to obtain your `ssh` information from alternative methods.

While on the topic of command-line utilities that are useful during development, we should discuss what's available from the shell session when you SSH into your gear using the `SSH:` line from the `rhc app show` or `rhc domain show` output. SSH access is permitted using the same keys that are set up and used along with the `rhc` utility. We could, of course, use `rhc ssh <application_name>` as a shorthand alternative for looking up the information, if we prefer. Commands available from the `ssh` shell on our gears are listed in the following table:

Shell command	Description
`ctl_app`	This command allows you to control your application's service daemon; you can start, stop, restart, gracefully restart, gracefully stop, and check the status where applicable.
`ctl_all`	This command allows you to perform the same functions as `ctl_app`, but it will also issue the same control command to the main application cartridge as well as all the currently embedded `addon` cartridges, wherever applicable.
`tail_all`	This command will accomplish the equivalent of performing `tail -f` on all applicable log files pertaining to a gear.
`export`	This will display all the currently defined environment variables within the gear currently SSH'd into.
`rm`	This is a command to remove files and directories; this is the GNU `rm` utility from coreutils.
`ls`	This command lists files and directories; this is the GNU `ls` utility from coreutils.
`ps`	Reports a snapshot of current processes. This is from the `procps-ng` project and accepts all the familiar command arguments.

Shell command	Description
`kill`	This command kills a currently running process; this kills the implementation from util-linux and is useful for dealing with hung processes.
`mysql, mongo, psql`	Each of these commands offer a direct access control interface for their respective databases.
`quota`	This command displays our current quota for disk space on the gear.

At this point, we have covered far and wide the materials that are needed to utilize OpenShift with the command-line client utilities, but one thing we must not do is neglect the other ways in which we can consume OpenShift and, as such, we will be moving on to the online web interface and then to IDE integrations.

Web Console

With the advent of modern web technologies such as HTML5, user interactions with the web have become more and more common, and that mindset is exactly what OpenShift aims to help developers deliver, or provide application administrators the ability to run. In this spirit, the OpenShift development team has written their own web user interface on which we can perform the following actions on applications:

- View
- Create
- Delete
- Restart
- Obtain detailed information

In this section, we will walk through the steps and show how to interact with the OpenShift Online web console.

 The OpenShift web console, just as the command-line utilities, is continuously undergoing active development, so certain views in the diagrams to follow are subject to change.

First, we will need to log in; then navigate to `https://openshift.com` with your favorite web browser and click on **MY APPS** at the top right. From there, we will be presented with a page similar to the following screenshot:

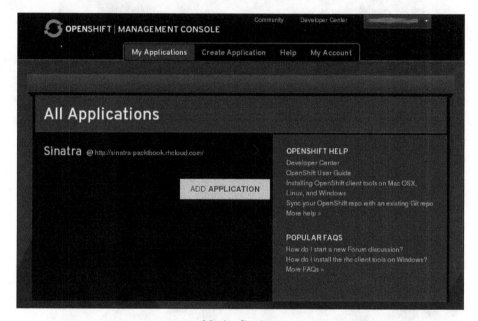

My Applications

The thing we should notice here in this layout is that we can see the application from the example in the *Command-line utilities* section of this chapter; if you followed along, you should see this as well when you log in. Now, since we created that application using the command-line tools, wrote a little code, and deployed it to the cloud, we should try out a different avenue of workflow for this example. What we'll do here is select the **ADD APPLICATION** option, shown in the preceding image, and we will be presented with the page found in the following screenshots, where screenshot A is what you'll find at the top, and screenshot B is what you'll find when you scroll down to the midsection; this was done for clarity:

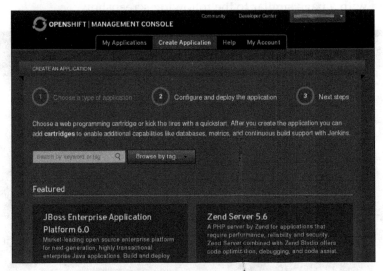

Screenshot A – Creating a new application

Screenshot B – Creating a new application

On this page, we find a multitude of options for deploying applications just as we did with command-line utilities. One thing to note in the preceding image is that we have a section named **Instant App**. While there is documentation on how to accomplish deploying these, and many more with the command-line utilities, this section of the interface offers us a one-click option to deploy. If we were to deploy these using command-line utilities, we would use what is known as the **QuickStarts** application (`https://www.openshift.com/developers/get-started`). Using the web console, we can deploy a number of the more popular of the QuickStarts instantly, hence, we use **Instant App**. Let's go ahead and select **Wordpress 3.4**, which will result in the automatic deployment of Wordpress, an extremely popular open source blogging and content management system (`http://wordpress.org/`). In the following screenshot, we are prompted to name the application just as we provided an application in the *Command-line utilities* section; for this example, I decided to be extremely creative and select the name `wordpress` as can be noted in the following screenshot. The following two screenshots are of the same web page but different sections; once again, this distinction is made for clarity. The latter of the two will be the bottom of the page where we select **Create Application**:

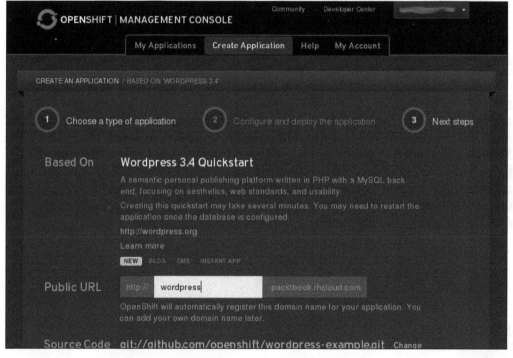

Screenshot A – Instant App, named Wordpress

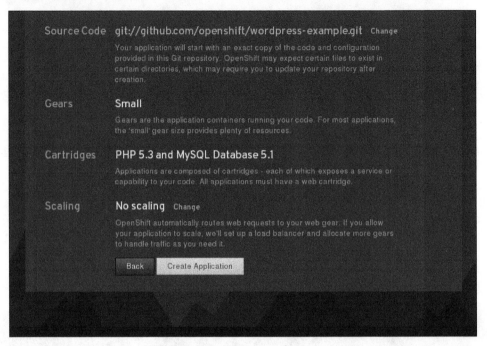

Screenshot B – Instant App, named Wordpress

In the spirit of openness, the OpenShift web console does not try to hide details away from us, the users. Instead, the console shows us details of what is happening behind the scenes. One example is the source code URL from where **Instant App** is being deployed, so that if we desired, we can Git clone the repository and see what makes all of this possible. Also, in the preceding image, it is mentioned that the **PHP 5.3 and MySQL Database 5.1** cartridges are used together; this is so that we are aware of the building blocks being used just as if we'd done so ourselves with the command-line utilities. Once we select **Create Application**, we will be presented with a screen that offers details about our database, how to access the application's gear, cloning our new Git repository, and more.

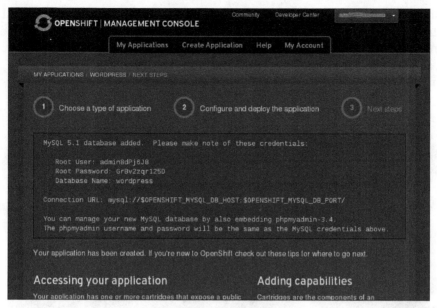

Application information

Now that our application is created, we have information about it and the methods to access it. If we were to return to the overview of our applications' listing, we would see both of the examples we have created so far, as shown in the following screenshot:

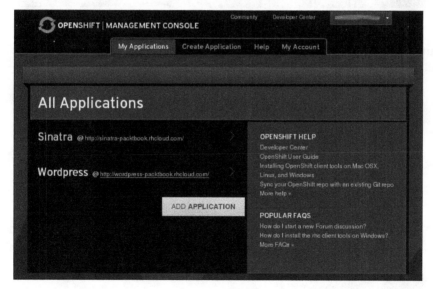

My Applications

From this dialog box, we can select the application we just created and view all the details as a reference point. There are some basic control functionalities also contained within this view of our application. One of these includes the ability to add another cartridge, such as phpmyadmin if we want a web interface to administer our database, as shown in the following screenshot:

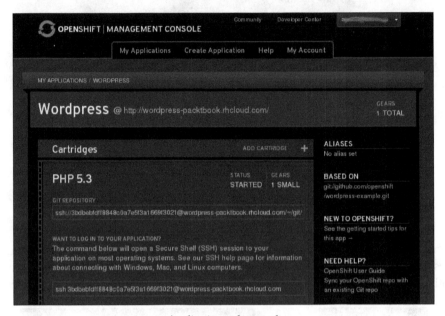

Application web control

Last, but not the least, let's visit our newly deployed **Wordpress** deployment:

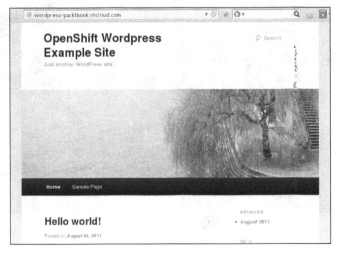

Wordpress

With our application deployed and the web application explored, it is now time to spend some time with **Integrated Development Environment (IDE)**, also known as JBoss Developer Studio.

IDE Integrations

Some developers enjoy their command-line editors, such as Vim or Emacs; some enjoy a graphical text editor targeted at developers, such as Gedit, Sublime Text, Kate, TextMate, or Notepad++, and others enjoy an IDE. An IDE is a piece of software used to develop software, often containing things such as build automation tools, debugging capabilities, compilers, interpreters, and often with a plugin ecosystem to provide extended functionality. Two examples of very popular IDEs are the Open Source IDE, named Eclipse, and Microsoft's Visual Studio. Continuing with the theme of offering developers as much choice as possible, not only does OpenShift offer command-line utilities and a web console, but also an IDE with built-in OpenShift capabilities named **JBoss Developer Studio (JBDS)** by Red Hat, which is based on the Open Source Eclipse IDE.

The first step is to download and install JBDS by following the instructions available at `https://devstudio.jboss.com/download/7.x.html`; once installed, we will be presented with a dialog box similar to the following screenshot:

JBoss Developer Studio – the Welcome tab

At this point, we should select **Getting Started**, and then we will see the JBDS workspace that contains a number of panels and toolbars. Of these, we will see **JBoss Central** in the center pane and inside this contains an entry titled **OpenShift Application**, as shown in the following screenshot:

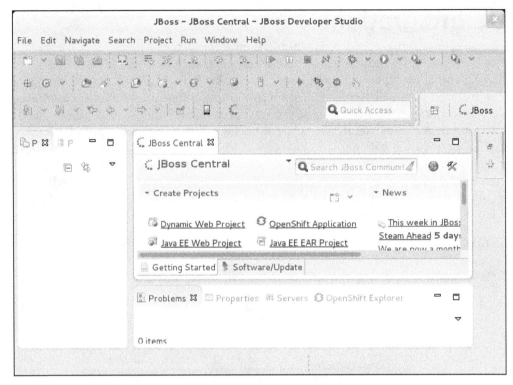

JBoss Developer Studio – the JBoss Central tab

Since we are using OpenShift, we of course want to select this option. Once this option is selected, we will enter our login information and password so that JBDS will communicate with the OpenShift Online servers to log in and provide our IDE with access to our applications. This is shown in the following screenshot:

JBoss Developer Studio – Sign in to OpenShift

 We could also have gone directly to import an existing application by navigating to **File** | **Import** | **OpenShift** | **Existing OpenShift Application**.

Once authenticated, we will be given the option to create a new application or use an existing application. For this example, we will select the option **Use an existing application:** and see how JBDS is able to access our account and import applications, as shown in the following screenshot:

JBoss Developer Studio – Setup OpenShift Application

Upon selecting the option to use existing applications and clicking on **Browse**, we are presented with a dialog box that shows the applications existing within our account in the OpenShift Online service. If we've been following along with the previous examples, there should be two applications already created, namely, **sinatra** and **wordpress**, as shown in the following screenshot:

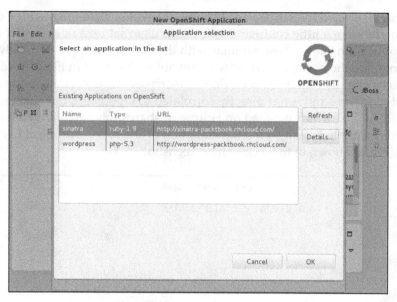

JBoss Developer Studio – selecting an application

Let's select the existing **sinatra** application. We do this because it is something we edited in a previous example and is considerably more simple than the code base for **wordpress**, which will make it easier for us to navigate, as shown in the following screenshot:

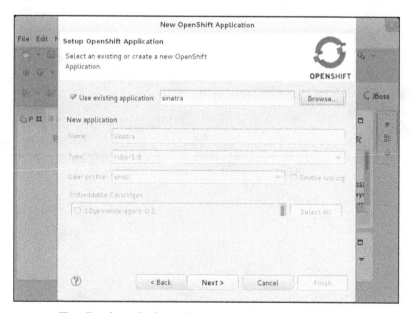

JBoss Developer Studio – selecting an application named Sinatra

Once we have selected the **sinatra** application, we will be presented with a dialog box that might seem a little confusing as it wants us to set up a new project for an existing application. Now, those familiar with the Eclipse IDE will not likely find this to be outside the norm, but those who are not well versed in Eclipse will likely find this to be slightly odd. However, do not worry as this is normal and the project is inherent to Eclipse and is not directly correlated to OpenShift, but since we are using the JBDS IDE, which is based on Eclipse, it shares this behavior. Due to the fact that this example is using a fresh installation of JBDS, we will select **Create a new project**, as shown in the following screenshot:

JBoss Developer Studio – creating a project

With the JBDS project in place, we will now point the IDE to our Git repository and can either import an existing project or use the remote branch. Because we've cloned previously using examples, we can use the local Git repository path and adopt its branch, as shown in the following screenshot:

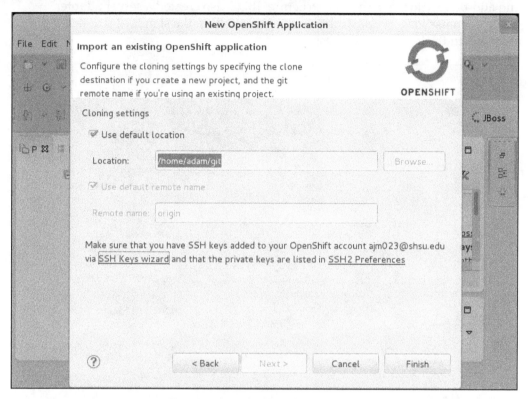

JBoss Developer Studio – Cloning settings

Once this selection is made, we will be brought back to a view of JBDS that is very similar to the one we've seen previously, but at this time, we will notice that in the left panel, our code repository has been imported. The account that we provided is now listed in the OpenShift Explorer, which will show accounts, applications, and add-on cartridges in the tree structure. JBDS also created a server adapter that we can use to easily push changes to OpenShift in the standard IDE fashion, as shown in the following screenshot:

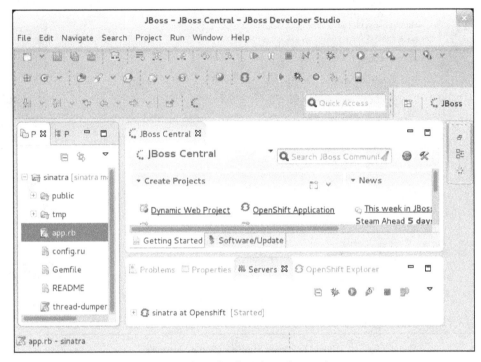

JBoss Developer Studio – the code repository

At this point, we can select a file, edit code, commit code to our local repository, and deploy it to OpenShift, all with the click of a button. This, of course, utilizes the server adapter mentioned previously.

Summary

Hopefully, we can select our preferred method of deploying on OpenShift, and developers of all backgrounds, preferences, and development platforms will feel at home working with OpenShift as a development and deployment platform. In *Chapter 3, OpenShift – Technologies and Working*, we will work through some details of how the OpenShift platform works internally as a service, discussing the different components and their individual roles within the service.

3
OpenShift – Technologies and Working

In *Chapter 2*, *Using OpenShift*, we discussed how to use OpenShift from an end user perspective, as a developer or web application administrator who might utilize OpenShift as an auto-scaling hosting environment. This chapter will take a deeper look into the technologies that drive OpenShift from the backend. The material we will cover in the following sections may not interest all parties, but those interested in what makes OpenShift tick should feel encouraged to read on and take a peek behind the curtains. Also, those who aim to deploy or host their own OpenShift Origin or Enterprise infrastructure, are likely find the information within the following sections of interest.

Before we delve too far into OpenShift nomenclature and inner workings, we should be sure and spend some time discussing the technologies that OpenShift relies upon. In the following sections, we cover what OpenShift utilizes in order to deliver its user experience, along with its unique architecture of Operating System level multitenancy. We will cover the following technologies in this chapter:

- Pluggable Authentication Modules for Linux
- SELinux
- Cgroups
- Software Collections
- Marionette Collective

These technologies are the building blocks upon which the unique architecture of OpenShift was built and we will spend some time with each one.

Pluggable Authentication Modules for Linux

The first technology we're going to discuss is **Pluggable Authentication Modules** (**PAM**) for Linux, which is a set of libraries that offers a single point of authentication for Linux-based operating systems. This is effectively the backend upon which privilege escalating utilities within the system will hand over the responsibility of authentication in a dynamic and configurable fashion. System administrators are able to modify the way different sessions and services authenticate the system using module configurations. Through the use of modules, PAM makes each of the following authentication functions separately configurable:

- Account management
- Authentication management
- Password management
- Session management

OpenShift uses this mechanism and has developed a custom PAM module that assists in providing the multitenant nature of OpenShift gears.

> The source code for the OpenShift PAM module is also available as part of the origin-server Git repository found at `https://github.com/openshift/origin-server`, for those who would like to dig into that source code.

Another PAM module heavily in use with OpenShift that assists in delivering the gear architecture is `pam_namespace`. It allows for each user or session to maintain its own namespace for directory structures, keeping one another from being able to view or impede upon one another's namespace. On the `pam_namespace.8` man page, the `pam_namespace` module is described such that,

> *"The pam_namespace PAM module sets up a private namespace for a session with polyinstantiated directories. A polyinstantiated directory provides a different instance of itself based on user name, or when using SELinux, user name, security context or both."*

Citations: *S. Smalley, J. Desai, C. Sellers, J. Desai, C. Sellers, S. Grubb, X. Toth, T. Mraz.*

This module is on how each OpenShift application's gear is able to have, for example, its own `/tmp/` directory and no other user, application, or Gear is able to access it. The example of how `/tmp/` functions are also delivered in parallel using the SELinux technology for enhanced security will be discussed under the *SELinux* heading in this chapter.

SELinux

The second technology we will spend some time covering in this chapter is called **Security Enhanced Linux (SELinux)**. This is a security technology originally developed by the United States National Security Agency to bring a heightened level of security capabilities to the Linux kernel. As an overview, this technology, best described as an upstream project at `http://www.nsa.gov/research/selinux/index.shtml` explains,

> *"NSA Security-enhanced Linux is a set of patches to the Linux kernel and some utilities to incorporate a strong, flexible mandatory access control (MAC) architecture into the major subsystems of the kernel. It provides an enhanced mechanism to enforce the separation of information based on confidentiality and integrity requirements, which allows threats of tampering and bypassing of application security mechanisms to be addressed and enables the confinement of damage that can be caused by malicious or flawed applications. It includes a set of sample security policy configuration files designed to meet common, general-purpose security goals."*

In a brief overview, SELinux will assign a set of contexts to files and processes, then use a set of policies that are defined in order to control transactions that can occur in the system between these contexts. This is how OpenShift limits different application's gears from being able to access parts of the system they should not be, such as the lower-level system and other application's gears running on the same node. Those interested in an in-depth look into SELinux are encouraged to explore the Red Hat SELinux guide available at `https://access.redhat.com/knowledge/docs/en-US/Red_Hat_Enterprise_Linux/6/html/Security-Enhanced_Linux/`.

CGroups

The Linux kernel contains a large number of features, one of which is **Control Groups (cgroups)**, which are kernel level constructs that allow for resource constraints. This is the mechanism upon which OpenShift is able to limit resources per application gear, and is combined with SELinux in order to offer the functionality of multitenancy at the Operating System level instead of relying on a form of virtualization or IaaS cloud.

For topics on Linux kernel documentation, there are a few places more authoritative than the official documentation that comes with the kernel source code; therefore, we shall refer to the discussion of cgroups definitions from a definite source:

"Definitions:

A *cgroup* associates a set of tasks with a set of parameters for one or more subsystems.

A *subsystem* is a module that makes use of the task grouping facilities provided by cgroups to treat groups of tasks in particular ways. A subsystem is typically a "resource controller" that schedules a resource or applies per-cgroup limits, but it may be anything that wants to act on a group of processes, e.g. a virtualization subsystem.

A *hierarchy* is a set of cgroups arranged in a tree, such that every task in the system is in exactly one of the cgroups in the hierarchy, and a set of subsystems; each subsystem has system-specific state attached to each cgroup in the hierarchy. Each hierarchy has an instance of the cgroup virtual filesystem associated with it.

At any one time there may be multiple active hierarchies of task cgroups. Each hierarchy is a partition of all tasks in the system.

User level code may create and destroy cgroups by name in an instance of the cgroup virtual file system, specify and query to which cgroup a task is assigned, and list the task pids assigned to a cgroup. Those creations and assignments only affect the hierarchy associated with that instance of the cgroup file system.

On their own, the only use for cgroups is for simple job tracking. The intention is that other subsystems hook into the generic cgroup support to provide new attributes for cgroups, such as accounting/limiting the resources which processes in a cgroup can access. For example, cpusets (see Documentation/cgroups/cpusets. txt) allows you to associate a set of CPUs and a set of memory nodes with the tasks in each cgroup."

The preceding quote is from the upstream Linux kernel documentation available at `https://www.kernel.org/doc/Documentation/cgroups/cgroups.txt`. Citations: *P. Menage, P.Jackson,C. Lameter.*

Software Collections

When working with GNU/Linux distributions, there are different life cycles of the code base contained in their package set, which can require special considerations for deployment of package sets that deviate from what is shipped in the official repository of our distribution. The examples of Enterprise Linux distributions are Red Hat Enterprise Linux, CentOS, and Scientific Linux, where the core operating system's package set is maintained to be stable, controlled, and predictable for the 10-year lifecycle of the code base. Refer to `https://access.redhat.com/support/policy/updates/errata/`. This comes with some implications based on how to effectively introduce updated package sets without compromising the stability and consistency of the core platform upon which we rely. This is where Software Collections come in. Software Collections is a system in which we can maintain namespaces for `rpm` package sets and enable them at will without affecting the system itself. This also allows for the ability to install multiple versions of the same software, such as an interpreted language in parallel, without impeding upon one another. As an example of this, we will demonstrate using the `scl` command-line utility to enable the Software Collection for `ruby 1.9.3` on a Red Hat Enterprise Linux 6 machine, as follows:

```
$ ruby -v
ruby 1.8.7 (2011-06-30 patchlevel 352) [x86_64-linux]
$ scl enable ruby193 bash
$ ruby -v
ruby 1.9.3p327 (2012-11-10 revision 37606) [x86_64-linux]
```

As can be seen from the preceding command output, we are able to change the running version of ruby without having to change any binary names in our commands or runtimes. Software Collections can also be used for any component within the system; at the time of writing this book, the upstream project hosted at FedoraHosted contained the SCL package repositories for `postgresql`, `python 3.x`, `ruby 1.9.3`, `httpd 2.4.x`, and many more. Those from DevOps and system administration backgrounds who maintain custom package repositories are encouraged to explore this topic in depth. But this brief introduction should be sufficient for explanations on how this technology fits into OpenShift in deployments through Red Hat Enterprise Linux and its cloned distributions, such as CentOS and Scientific Linux. More information on SCL can be found at the following resources:

- `https://fedoraproject.org/wiki/SoftwareCollections`
- `https://fedorahosted.org/SoftwareCollections/`
- `https://access.redhat.com/site/documentation/en-US/Red_Hat_Developer_Toolset/1/html/Software_Collections_Guide/`

MCollective

Marionette Collective (**MCollective**) is an open source framework for server orchestration and parallel job execution across an environment of distributed systems, written and developed by Puppet Labs. It leverages either STOMP compliant or AMQP message-passing mechanisms in the background, and provides an easy-to-use and consistent set of commands, as well as an API that will assist in the facilitation of almost anything needed between a distributed set of servers. More information about MCollective can be found at `http://docs.puppetlabs.com/mcollective/index.html`.

 Popular examples of STOMP or AMQP message-passing mechanisms are ActiveMQ (`https://activemq.apache.org/`), RabbitMQ (`http://www.rabbitmq.com/`), and QPID (`https://qpid.apache.org/`).

Applications and Gears

With an understanding of the background technologies that provide a functionality offered in OpenShift, we need to revisit the notion of applications and gears. When we use command-line client utilities, a web administration console, or IDE integration to create an application, it creates one or many gears for our **Application**. Remembering that this **Gear** is a resource container constrained with cgroups and confined by SELinux, we can conceptually think of this as our "slice" of the Operating System; within this slice will be our cartridges. We've covered cartridges previously, but as a reminder, these are effectively the puzzle pieces with which we assemble the platform for our web applications, such as language runtimes, databases, and the plugin functionality. A single OpenShift application can consume multiple OpenShift gears in different scenarios, the most common of which is in the situation of an auto-scaling event. The following diagram demonstrates this relationship:

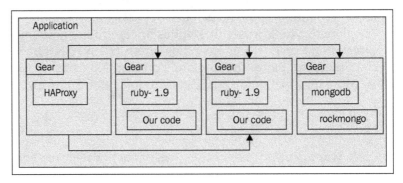

Applications and Gears, a scaled-out example

In the preceding diagram, we have a single application that is currently scaled out, meaning that an **HAProxy** gear is spawned, the second gear of our application and second copy of our code is spawned, and all the application web requests will, from that point through the HAProxy node with requests, load balance between the other application gears.

The OpenShift architecture overview

The preceding diagram offers an overview of the OpenShift architecture. In the following sections, we will be discussing how each component fits together and how they function. At this point, we should travel through a workflow and visit the different points along the path our code travels, and take small detours from the main data flow in order to spend time covering events that occur along the way, as follows:

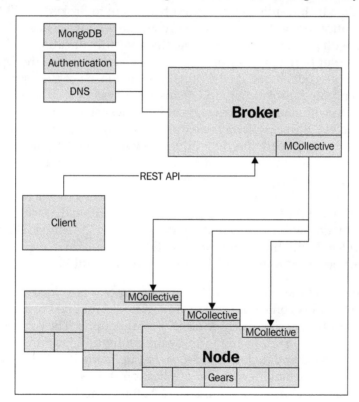

OpenShift architecture

At the starting point, we would be using some sort of end user interface of the OpenShift service and for the sake of the example, let's assume that choice is the command-line client utilities. When we run an `rhc` command, the utilities on the backend make a **REST API** call to **Broker** as Broker is the central point of orchestration for the service.

 We will discuss REST API in a later section.

Let's take a moment to walk through an example of an action we would perform with the `rhc` command-line utility and discuss what will happen on the backend of our OpenShift infrastructure. When we create an OpenShift application using the `rhc app create -a myapp -t ruby-1.9` command, the client utilities make a REST API call, which results in the request being sent to Broker; it will first check with our authentication backend to make sure we are who we claim to be, or at least someone with proper credentials. Note that the authentication backend can be configured to support a number of different mechanisms using the OpenShift origin or enterprise code, based on the plugins available. Once the user request is properly authenticated, Broker will update the **DNS** system to propagate the name of the application within our OpenShift domain namespace. At the point the DNS creation is complete, Broker will traverse through an algorithm that will select **Node** with the least amount of load; this determines how populated Node is, which types of **Cartridges** are deployed on it, and the usage analytics. Node selected from this algorithm will be the one upon which a new Gear will be created for our Application to consume. With the selection made, Broker will instruct Node via **MCollective** to perform the task of the Gear creation containing Cartridge that we've selected. The Gear information will, at this point, be stored within the **MongoDB** data store as well as correlated with the account information to maintain mapping of the user to the domain, and to determine which applications live within the user's domain.

In order to construct Gear on Node, the following process is followed: a unique ID is generated, a SELinux context is created, and these are mapped to a traditional UNIX-style ID for the specific machine Gear is created upon. The container is set up with the resource constraints put forth by the configurations for the Gear sizes using cgroups. Polyinstantiated directories are set up using PAM and they adhere to the SELinux policies, making sure our application stays within its confines, as well as to keep other applications out of our space. At the point the container setup is complete, Cartridge will be installed based on the cartridge's YAML manifest. These manifests can be found in the upstream `github` repository under the listing for each of the cartridges. At this point, we are able to SSH into our Gear and the prompt we would be presented with is a limited shell within this environment.

YAML is a data serialization standard. For more information, visit http://www.yaml.org/.

Since we're now familiar with how to create an application, we should map the flow of traffic within OpenShift once we have **Gears** up and running. A web request will come out from somewhere in cyberspace, it will go to whichever Node that our application's DNS pointer happens to point to, and it will hit Node and be routed through a proxy (more on this shortly). In the event our Gear is running, the request will be received and our application will respond to it. However, in the event that our application has not received traffic within a certain span of time, it will be put into an "idle" state by OpenShift in order to reclaim resources previously used by the application.

If our application has been "idled" due to extended inactivity, the request will be caught by a proxy component of the OpenShift Node, our Gear will be brought out of the idled state, and the request will be passed on to it. It should also be noted that within the nodes, there is a set of internal IP addresses and ports for services versus external IP addresses and ports; these are part of the gear's metadata that is orchestrated by Broker based on Cartridge in use, and these attributes are set within Gears, using the environment variables we discussed in previous sections.

Previously, in *Chapter 2, Using OpenShift*, we briefly mentioned environment variables within our gear; these exist in a set of files within the ~/.env/ directory on the gear and those that are in use are populated as needed. The environment variables available to our gear at the time of writing are as follows:

```
HISTFILE                      OPENSHIFT_MONGODB_DB_PORT

OPENSHIFT_APP_DNS               OPENSHIFT_MONGODB_DB_URL

OPENSHIFT_APP_NAME              OPENSHIFT_MONGODB_DB_USERNAME

OPENSHIFT_APP_UUID              OPENSHIFT_NODEJS_IP

OPENSHIFT_DATA_DIR              OPENSHIFT_NODEJS_LOG_DIR

OPENSHIFT_GEAR_DNS              OPENSHIFT_NODEJS_PORT

OPENSHIFT_GEAR_NAME           OPENSHIFT_REPO_DIR

OPENSHIFT_GEAR_UUID             OPENSHIFT_ROCKMONGO_IP

OPENSHIFT_HOMEDIR             OPENSHIFT_ROCKMONGO_LOG_DIR

OPENSHIFT_INTERNAL_IP               OPENSHIFT_ROCKMONGO_PORT

OPENSHIFT_INTERNAL_PORT          OPENSHIFT_TMP_DIR

OPENSHIFT_MONGODB_DB_HOST        PATH

OPENSHIFT_MONGODB_DB_LOG_DIR     USER_VARS

OPENSHIFT_MONGODB_DB_PASSWORD
```

Some of these are important to understand some of the inner workings of the OpenShift traffic flow. A gear is given internal and external ports for different services and components. The internal versions map behind the scenes in order to allow each gear to bind to ports as needed, and these are mapped to a random port on the node itself, and set into a reverse proxy configuration so that the outside world can access the application based on the DNS name and its services' default ports. All of this port abstraction and orchestration is handled automatically by OpenShift and does not need to be the concern of application developers or web app users, but instead can be utilized by referencing any one of these environment variables. Details of which of the environment variables may be pertinent to our application are contained in the README file associated with the cartridge that we selected.

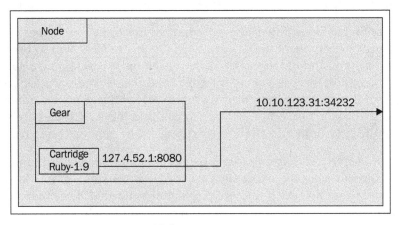

Node reverse proxy

In the preceding diagram, we can see that the OpenShift **Gear** to **Node** port mapping is relatively random in terms of which port is held by the Gear mapping, but what occurs behind the scenes is that an HAProxy (`http://haproxy.1wt.eu/`) rule is put in place for the Virtual Host, which points to our Gear on Node so that requests are routed correctly to our web app. This intra-gear networking is accomplished using the proper implementation of Linux kernel's **RFC 3330** in respect to the loopback network (`http://tools.ietf.org/html/rfc3330`). This allows us to route all the IP addresses within the loopback IP space locally on the host without assigning them to an interface. However, OpenShift takes it one step further and applies the iptables (`http://www.netfilter.org/projects/iptables/index.html`) firewall rules on Node to isolate traffic within the loopback network properly. This is done to stop the gears that should not communicate from communicating.

To sum up, Broker is the control point or the "brains of the operation", such that it orchestrates the rest of the environment to act on the user's behalf via REST API. Broker is responsible for DNS entries, user authentication, account metadata mapping, gear creation and deletion (delegation to the nodes via MCollective), and gear distribution across nodes. Node is responsible for running Gear, mapping its components to an application, idling and un-idling gears based upon load, and collectively keeping the underlying technologies we've discussed previously configured automatically for each Gear.

The REST API

In the previous sections, we have mentioned a REST API in passing, but we will now explore the topic. For those not familiar, **REST API** is an acronym for **Representational State Transfer Application Programming Interface**. This is a model in which a request of a URL constitutes a state transition, and the response from the server after processing this request is a representation of the resource that exists at the other end of the URL. The REST model is closely related to HTTP capabilities and mirrors its functions, such as GET, POST, PUT, and DELETE. Using this, we are able to interact with our service or resource without a hard requirement on a specific programming language binding, because as long as there's an HTTP capability, we are able to utilize the API. Almost all programming languages have this built-in functionality and it even allows us to utilize resources via command-line utilities that provide HTTP functionalities, such as curl.

We will use the curl utility in order to do an introduction to the OpenShift REST API, so the first thing we want to do is see what is available as resources from the service as follows:

```
$ curl -k -X GET \
   https://openshift.redhat.com/broker/rest/api
```

```
{"data":{"API":{"href":"https://openshift.redhat.com/broker/
rest/api","method":"GET","optional_params":[],"rel":"API entry
point","required_params":[]},"GET_ENVIRONMENT":{"href":"https://
openshift.redhat.com/broker/rest/environment","method":"GET","op
tional_params":[],"rel":"Get environment information","required_
params":[]},"GET_USER":{"href":"https://openshift.redhat.com/broker/
rest/user","method":"GET","optional_params":[],"rel":"Get user
information","required_params":[]},"LIST_DOMAINS":{"href":"https://
openshift.redhat.com/broker/rest/domains","method":"GET","optio
nal_params":[],"rel":"List domains","required_params":[]},"ADD_
DOMAIN":{"href":"https://openshift.redhat.com/broker/rest/domains","me
thod":"POST","optional_params":[],"rel":"Create new domain","required_
params":[{"description":"Name of the domain","invalid_options":["amentra"
,"aop","apiviz","arquillian","blacktie","boxgrinder","byteman","cirras","
cloud","cloudforms","cygwin","davcache","dogtag","drools","drools","e
```

```
jb3","errai","esb","fedora","freeipa","gatein","git","gfs","gravel","guv
nor","hibernate","hornetq","iiop","infinispan","ironjacamar","javassist"
,"jbcaa","jbcd","jboss","jbpm","jdcom","jgroups","jmx","jopr","jrunit","
jsfunit","kosmos","liberation","makara","mass","maven","metajizer","meta
matrix","mobicents","mod_cluster","modeshape","mugshot","mysql","netty",
"openshift","osgi","overlord","ovirt","penrose","picketbox","picketlink"
,"portletbridge","portletswap","posse","pressgang","qumranet","railo","r
edhat","resteasy","rhca","rhcds","rhce","rhcsa","rhcss","rhct","rhcva","
rhel","rhev","rhq","rhx","richfaces","riftsaw","savara","scribble","seam
","shadowman","shotoku","shrinkwrap","snowdrop","solidice","spacewalk","
spice","steamcannon","stormgrind","switchyard","tattletale","teiid","toh
u","torquebox","weld","wise","xnio"],"name":"id","type":"string","valid_
options":[]}]},"LIST_CARTRIDGES":{"href":"https://openshift.redhat.com/
broker/rest/cartridges","method":"GET","optional_params":[],"rel":"List
cartridges","required_params":[]},"LIST_QUICKSTARTS":{"href":"https://
openshift.redhat.com/community/api/v1/quickstarts/promoted.
json","method":"GET","optional_params":[],"rel":"List
quickstarts","required_params":[]},"SHOW_QUICKSTART":{"href":"https://
openshift.redhat.com/community/api/v1/quickstarts/:id","method":"GET"
,"optional_params":[],"rel":"Retrieve quickstart with :id","required_
params":[{"description":"Unique identifier of the quickstart","invalid_op
tions":[],"name":":id","type":"string","valid_options":[]}]},"SEARCH_
QUICKSTARTS":{"href":"https://openshift.redhat.com/community/api/v1/
quickstarts.json","method":"GET","optional_params":[],"rel":"Search
quickstarts","required_params":[{"description":"The search term to use
for the quickstart","invalid_options":[],"name":"search","type":"string",
"valid_options":[]}]}},"messages":[],"status":"ok","supported_api_version
s":[1.0,1.1,1.2,1.3],"type":"links","version":"1.3"}
```

 This output is in the **JSON** format, which stands for **JavaScript Object Notation** and it has become a staple format in web technologies for data transmission. For more information, please visit http://json.org/.

In the preceding output, we have sent a request to the REST API at its root, which will provide us with information about the resources available to us, as well as information about which versions of the REST API are currently supported. You have probably noticed that the preceding command looks garbled. For the sake of sanity, I suggest using the following command to pipe the output from curl to a simple python call:

```
curl -k X \
    GET"https://openshift.redhat.com/broker/rest/api" | python -mjson.
pretty
```

The preceding command assumes you have python installed. If you are using either Mac OS X or a popular distribution of GNU/ Linux, such as Fedora, Debian, OpenSUSE, Arch, or Ubuntu, you are most likely to already have this installed. If you are running Windows or are unfamiliar with python, it is recommended to visit `http://www.python.org/` for more information, both on the python programming language as well as the installation instructions.

The output of the `curl` command in the preceding command was omitted in its entirety for brevity, as the end result is quite verbose. The following is a short sample of what the formatting would look like when running a JSON "pretty print":

```
"API": {
        "href": "https://openshift.redhat.com/broker/rest/api",
        "method": "GET",
        "optional_params": [],
        "rel": "API entry point",
        "required_params": []
    },
    "GET_ENVIRONMENT": {
        "href": "https://openshift.redhat.com/broker/rest/
environment",
        "method": "GET",
        "optional_params": [],
        "rel": "Get environment information",
        "required_params": []
    },
    "GET_USER": {
        "href": "https://openshift.redhat.com/broker/rest/user",
        "method": "GET",
        "optional_params": [],
        "rel": "Get user information",
        "required_params": []
    },
    "LIST_CARTRIDGES": {
        "href": "https://openshift.redhat.com/broker/rest/
cartridges",
        "method": "GET",
```

```
        "optional_params": [],
        "rel": "List cartridges",
        "required_params": []
    },
    "LIST_DOMAINS": {
        "href": "https://openshift.redhat.com/broker/rest/domains",
        "method": "GET",
        "optional_params": [],
        "rel": "List domains",
        "required_params": []
    },
    "LIST_QUICKSTARTS": {
        "href": "https://openshift.redhat.com/community/api/v1/
quickstarts/promoted.json",
        "method": "GET",
        "optional_params": [],
        "rel": "List quickstarts",
        "required_params": []
    },
```

While this output is certainly more easy on the eyes, its considerably more long-winded, so a large portion of it has been left out. Something to note here though is that, by running the GET function on the main API URL, we are able to explore other parts of the API; you will see here that the functionality we are interested in is written all in caps, such as LIST_DOMAINS. In order to obtain that resource, we would use the URL described in the "href" portion of the object, which is https://openshift.redhat.com/broker/rest/domains. If we are to run the curl command from our previous example using a GET function and our username and password combination, we would see the following output, which is obtainable from that resource:

```
$ curl -k -X GET https://openshift.redhat.com/broker/rest/domains --user
"myuser@example.com:mypassword" | python -mjson.pretty


### Output omitted for brevity


"LIST_APPLICATIONS": {
                "href": "https://openshift.redhat.com/broker/rest/
domains/mydomain/applications",
```

```
        "method": "GET",

        "optional_params": [],

        "rel": "List applications",

        "required_params": []

    },
```

Now, we can see in the snippet of the preceding output that we're able to obtain an application listing within our domain. If we were to look back at our `rhc` command-line utility and run the `rhc domain show` command, it would provide us with a certain amount of information about our domain, the applications within it, and the cartridges within our applications. We can obtain this data from the command line using the `curl` utility, along with the URL listed in the `"href"` section of the object, to obtain some insight as to what the command-line client does for us by abstracting away the raw REST API into a user-friendly utility, by using the following command:

```
$ curl -k -X GET \

https://openshift.redhat.com/broker/rest/domains/mydomain/applications   \

    --user "myusername@example.com:mypassword"
```

The output from this command is quite long. When run against my domain and sent through the python command from our previous example to "pretty print" the JSON, the line count of the output was `1010`, and therefore it too has been omitted in order to not waste unnecessary page space with JSON outputs. If you've followed along, you should have more of an insight into how to interact with the OpenShift service via its REST APIs and how these requests get processed internally by the different OpenShift components. The REST API itself is, however, continuing to evolve, which is why there is a section that notates a supported version of the API so that different versions may be selected. So, it is always advisable to consult the upstream documentation to see what has changed. For more information, it would be beneficial to visit `https://access.redhat.com/knowledge/docs/OpenShift/` and select the **REST API Guide** option for information on the latest version.

Summary

In this chapter, we have explored what makes OpenShift tick, covering the technologies upon which it depends, such as SELinux, Cgroups, and in some deployments, Software Collections. From there, we looked at an overview of the OpenShift architecture and broke it down piece by piece to discuss how each component works in its own right, as well as all together in order to make a fully functional platform. This level of understanding will be extremely helpful as we move forward to the next chapter and discuss topics of DevOps and automated deployment.

4
Deploying an OpenShift PaaS

Leading up to this point, we have focused pretty heavily on an end user or a developer perspective of OpenShift. Even discussions surrounding the OpenShift architecture, internal components, and walking through the flow of data through the environment is helpful to developers in understanding what's happening behind the scenes of the platform upon which they rely. While the journey through the architecture was invaluable to those of us in Systems Administration, Operations, or DevOps roles, it was not primarily focused on that audience, but it will change as we move forward. This chapter will be used as a resource not only for deploying OpenShift, but also for providing different avenues that can be taken by those who wish to work with their very own open source PaaS. Once again, note that this can be done with physical hardware, virtual machines, or cloud instances running on an IaaS cloud. Since we will be deploying on our own systems, we will be using the upstream open source code base known as **OpenShift Origin**.

As mentioned previously, there are multiple ways through which we can consume OpenShift Origin. At the time of this writing, we are able to install OpenShift Origin using:

- Nightly built rpm package sets from the upstream project
- Packages available in the Fedora Project rpm repository
- The upstream source code

We will first take a moment to discuss OpenShift Origin and Fedora along with a little history and future plans surrounding their relationships with the greater open source community. After that, we will talk about installing Fedora inside a virtual machine using an open source virtualization technology called **Kernel Based Virtual Machine (KVM)**. For more info, check `http://www.linux-kvm.org`. Before we delve too deep into these topics, it must be pointed out that the subject of deployment certainly falls within the DevOps realm and we will be utilizing a tool that certainly fits well within that topic space. One of the most powerful tools in the DevOps tool chain is a configuration management system combined with the capability to perform server orchestration, and sometimes we're fortunate that a single utility offers both. The tool we will use in this section to perform the deployment of OpenShift Origin is called **Ansible** and we will discuss it shortly, but first let's talk a bit about the Fedora Project.

The Fedora Project

The Fedora Project has been mentioned briefly in the earlier sections but we will spend some time discussing the relationship between OpenShift and the Fedora Project. We will also cover their relationship with a broader community of contributors or potential contributors around the world. Contributors in this sense are those who participate in open source to help advance Free/Libre open source software and innovate it more rapidly in a collaborative manner. The Fedora Project aims to be a central hub in which like-minded developers, technologists, enthusiasts, designers, technical writers, makers, innovators, thinkers, and general fans can come together and help one another foster an environment in which open source software can flourish. The Fedora Project is a community-powered and governed project that is sponsored by Red Hat Inc. The Fedora Project members power a large number of community subprojects in the realm of documentation, design, technical evangelists (known as Fedora Ambassadors—`https://fedoraproject.org/wiki/Ambassadors`), and many other Special Interest Groups (`https://fedoraproject.org/wiki/Category:SIGs?rd=SIGs`).

Fedora is a project where **upstream** is the key. It is a premier place for projects such as OpenShift Origin to spend time in getting their code, community exposure, interests, and welcome new community members, users, and contributors. The Fedora Project has a reputation for not only its ongoing upstream contributions, such that code does not traditionally make it into the Fedora repositories without first being contributed to the upstream project from where it originated, but also for its belief in the value of free software. As many people come into the Fedora Project from the external world, they are greeted by the Fedora Core Values:

- Freedom
- Friends

- Features
- First

One of the main things that the Fedora Project produces is the **Fedora GNU/Linux** distribution; it is the basis for **Red Hat Enterprise Linux** and these will often share common technologies. Something to note about the differences found within these two distributions of GNU/Linux is that Fedora is very focused on the latest and greatest available in software technologies and will often track the most up-to-date versions of open source software. Fedora developers will either choose to ship these by default on a fresh installation or have it available for download in the rpm repositories utilizing the **yum package manager** (or optionally, other compatible package managers).

The Yum package manager is the default package manager used by both the Fedora and Red Hat Enterprise Linux operating systems, but alternatives for these systems do exist. These package managers are used to track software installed in the system as well as dependencies thereof, much like we saw with the Gem utility in previous sections. But they are considerably more powerful in that they are not limited to RubyGems. Those not familiar with yum are encouraged to seek more information for the upstream project from `http://yum.baseurl.org/`.

The Fedora GNU/Linux distribution aims to deliver cutting-edge technology and always pushes the envelope on next generation technologies, which releases a new version every six months and maintains approximately a one-year lifecycle per release. A lifecycle in the context of a GNU/Linux distribution is effectively how long from the point in time it is released it will continue to receive software updates for security and bug fixes. The Red Hat Enterprise Linux distribution is aimed towards environments where stability and length of life cycle is desired and, at the time of this writing, offers a 10-year default life cycle. However, due to the areas where technologies are shared and the fact that Red Hat Enterprise Linux receives what are known as **backports** that deliver features (`https://access.redhat.com/support/policy/updates/errata/`), both of these offer the software requirements that we have discussed in previous sections, such as SELinux, cgroups, and pam_namespaces, so we are able to use either of these as a basis to deploy OpenShift upon.

A reason we've appeared to become derailed from the topic of OpenShift and on into a segment about Fedora is because this is the chosen upstream GNU/Linux distribution upon which OpenShift Origin is actively developed. Also at the time of this writing, OpenShift Origin is an official feature of Fedora and it can be installed from the official Fedora Repositories. Please refer to `https://fedoraproject.org/wiki/OpenShift_Origin` for more information about this inclusion and to check all the available options through the official Fedora Repositories.

Since we will be using Fedora as our deployment platform for OpenShift Origin, we will need to have it installed on some hardware, in a virtual machine, or in an IaaS cloud instance somewhere. I will show you an example of how to perform an automated deployment using **QEMU-KVM** (http://www.linux-kvm.org/page/Main_Page, http://wiki.qemu.org/KVM) and a Fedora installer technology called **Kickstart** (https://fedoraproject.org/wiki/Anaconda/Kickstart). If this example does not fit for your exact configuration, there are a multitude of ways in which to consume Fedora, much of which can be found at the following resources:

- https://fedoraproject.org/wiki/Fedora_Quick_Install_Guide
- http://docs.fedoraproject.org/en-US/Fedora/19/html/Installation_Guide/index.html
- http://fedoraproject.org/en/get-fedora-options#cloud

In the following example, OpenShiftOrigin is the virtual machine's name, but first we need to install the virtualization components on our Fedora machine. Again, we're assuming that we are running Fedora GNU/Linux at this point:

```
$ yum -y install @virtualization
$ service libvirtd start
$ chkconfig libvirtd on
$ virsh net-define /usr/share/libvirt/networks/default.xml
$ virsh net-start default
```

In the preceding series of commands, we have run what is known as a **Group Install** of the virtualization packages for Fedora, then started the libvirtd service, as well as checked to make sure it will start automatically when we boot our machine. From there we've used the libvirt command-line utility known as virsh to define our default network using the default config that comes with libvirt, as well as started that network. Please note that we've just taken a whirlwind approach to virtualization on Fedora, but that's only for the sake of brevity so that we can move on to the main course, that is, deploying OpenShift Origin. It is recommended for anyone not familiar with the steps that just took place to pursue more information from the Fedora Documentation Project on the topic of virtualization, which can be found at https://docs.fedoraproject.org/en-US/Fedora/19/html/Virtualization_Getting_Started_Guide/index.html.

Next up we will be performing the installation of Fedora using all the wonderful automation tools. Our virtual machine will be given a 15 GB hard drive image, 2 vCPUS (not necessary, but helps speed up the process), and 2 GB of RAM. There is not a hard requirement on RAM but it is recommended to have 2 GB as a minimum, and the number of active Gears you can run simultaneously will depend on the amount of RAM your system has. Following is a code snippet for this purpose:

```
$ image_name="OpenShiftOrigin"
$ image_path=/opt/$image_name

$ qemu-img create "$image_path" 15G -f raw
$ parted "$image_path" mklabel msdos
$ parted --align optimal "$image_path" mkpart primary ext4 1M 15G
$ mkfs.ext4 -F "$image_path"

$ kickstart_args='ks=http://maxamillion.fedorapeople.org/base-
fedora-19.cfg'

$ virt-install --name="$image_name" --ram=2048 --vcpus=2 --hvm \
  --disk "$image_path" --graphics spice -d --wait=-1 --autostart \
  --location http://mirrors.kernel.org/fedora/releases/19/Fedora/
x86_64/os/ \
  -x "$kickstart_args" --connect qemu:///system --network
network=default
```

Let's take a moment to walk through what's happening in the preceding example. First, we're assigning two variables `image_name` and `image_path`, which will contain the Virtual Machine's name and the path to its virtual image on our host's local disk, respectively. Next we are using the `qemu-img` command to create a raw image that is 15 GB in size. At this point, we will use the GNU-parted utility to partition this image so that it is suitable for a filesystem to be created upon.

We could technically create a filesystem directly on a raw image but normally the OS installer will prefer that we have a more traditional layout. It should also be noted that this automated configuration is extremely simple and should be used for testing or development purposes.

Once we have our partition created, we will then set the kickstart parameters that will be needed for the following, very large, single command that will work along with libvirt (http://libvirt.org/) in order to define a virtual machine domain, offer it networking capabilities using the default virtual network as defined within libvirt, and begin the installation of a virtual machine. This process will be very verbose in your terminal window, and if you have X11 installed with some sort of Desktop Environment up and running, it will also launch what is known as virt-viewer so that we may watch the installation process. This graphical window will be showing a text-based prompt too and you will see the output of the automated install scroll by. Once the initial download of the packages is complete, you will be prompted with the Anaconda installer, which will show the installation and will look like the following screenshot:

```
OpenShiftOrigin (1) - Virt Viewer (on mobileshift)          ⊗

  File  View  Send key  Help

Starting installer, one moment...
anaconda 18.37.11 for Fedora 18 started.
Starting automated install.
Generating updated storage configuration
Checking storage configuration...
You have not specified a swap partition.  Although not strictly required in all
cases, it will significantly improve performance for most installations.
================================================================================
================================================================================
Install hub

 1) [x] Timezone settings              2) [x] Install Destination
        (America/Chicago timezone)            (Custom partitioning selected)
 3) [x] Set root password
        (Password is set.)
================================================================================
================================================================================
Installation Hub
Creating disklabel on /dev/vda
.
Creating ext4 on /dev/vda1
.
Starting package installation process

[anaconda] 1:main* 2:shell  3:log  4:storage-log  5:program-log
```

Fedora 19 Kickstart install

> The root password for this example kickstart installation is openshift! and should be changed immediately after installation is complete if this is to be used for more than just an example environment.

Once this is complete, the virtual machine will reboot and we will be presented with a login prompt, and then we're ready to get moving with our OpenShift Origin deployment. First things first, and that will be to configure the network within our Virtual Machine. To do so, edit the file `/etc/sysconfig/network-scripts/ifcfg-eth0` such that it reflects the following:

```
DEVICE=eth0
HWADDR=52:54:00:fc:62:cd
BOOTPROTO=static
NM_CONTROLLED=yes
IPADDR=192.168.122.10
NETMASK=255.255.255.0
DNS1=192.168.122.1
GATEWAY=192.168.122.1
ONBOOT=yes
```

Save this file and run the following command that will restart the `NetworkManager` service putting our configuration into effect:

```
service NetworkManager restart
```

> The HWADDR in your config is going to be different than what is found in the preceding example and should be left set to what it was set during installation. There also may be a field titled UUID, and if this is present it should also be left alone.

At this point our environment is set up and ready to move on, and this will be used as the platform upon which we deploy OpenShift Origin. As an aside, hopefully we've covered enough of the Fedora Project so that those who are reading about it for the first time have an added interest in learning more. We've outlined the relationship between the OpenShift Origin project and that of Fedora in a way that hopefully everyone is comfortable with understanding, and we are now ready to perform some deployment of OpenShift Origin using the Fedora GNU/Linux distribution as our host operating system.

Ansible

Ansible (`https://github.com/ansible/ansible`) is a simple, yet advanced, open source system orchestration utility that offers the ability to run ad-hoc commands across a large number of hosts in parallel, to orchestrate sets of commands, as well as configure management. Ansible has a very large set of modules for automating a multitude of tasks (`http://www.ansibleworks.com/docs/modules.html`). When utilizing a module to perform something, this is known as a **Task**, as we will learn shortly. We can combine these Tasks into what is known in Ansible nomenclature as a **Play** and these can be combined into what Ansible calls **Playbooks**. We can then run Playbooks using the `ansible-playbook` command. For those in the DevOps arena unfamiliar with Ansible, fear not as it is the new kid on the block and easy to learn, as we will see shortly. Now, don't let the fact that Ansible is new be a cause for concern as the open source project won the **Black Duck Open Source Rookie of the Year 2012** award (`http://www.wired.com/wiredenterprise/2013/01/open-source-rookies-of-year/`) and is backed by a startup known as AnsibleWorks (`http://www.ansibleworks.com/`), for those interested in seeking support and services.

Some interesting points about Ansible that should be noted early on are that we don't need to introduce a new specific daemon to run Ansible as it utilizes SSH, which everyone reading this book should at least be familiar with as we have covered it in *Chapter 1, Understanding the Essentials*. We don't need to open another port in our firewalls because if we can SSH into our servers, we can run Ansible on them. Ansible also does not require us to learn any sort of programming language or domain-specific language in order to create very powerful configuration automation, as it uses very simple YAML (`http://www.yaml.org/`) files paired with its running list of modules. One last thing to note about Ansible before we dig in is that its actions are **idempotent**, meaning that if we run the same action over and over, it should always leave the system in the same state as it did the first time we performed that action.

Let's go ahead, dive in, and start getting our hands dirty, and we will learn some "Intro to Ansible" along the way. Since we're only going to be using Fedora for the duration of this section, we will first want to install Ansible by running the following command as root:

```
yum -y install ansible
```

If you prefer to run Ansible from a different operating system and have set up a Fedora Virtual Machine on your own for the duration of this example, please consult the AnsibleWorks site for installation instructions: http://www.ansibleworks. com/docs/gettingstarted.html.

Once installed, if we are to use the example environment we just set up with the automated deployment kickstart utility, we will have a couple of setup tasks; first, we will need to generate SSH keys (those who already have a set of SSH keys feel free to skip this step):

```
$ ssh-keygen
Generating public/private rsa key pair.
Enter file in which to save the key (/root/.ssh/id_rsa):
Created directory '/root/.ssh'.
Enter passphrase (empty for no passphrase):
Enter same passphrase again:
Your identification has been saved in /root/.ssh/id_rsa.
Your public key has been saved in /root/.ssh/id_rsa.pub.
The key fingerprint is:
df:8c:88:79:75:40:82:71:72:bd:8c:43:09:ab:b1:b5 root@localhost.
localdomain
The key's randomart image is:
+--[ RSA 2048]----+
|       ++++o.     |
|       .=oo.      |
|     . o. o..     |
|      = .o o.     |
|     o E S.. .    |
|        o + =     |
|        o o o o   |
|          .       |
|                  |
+-----------------+
```

With our SSH key in place, we will want to use the `ssh-copy-id` utility in order to copy it over to our virtual machine so that we can perform key-based authentication for the duration of our use case. We will do so by running the following command:

```
$ ssh-copy-id root@192.168.122.10
The authenticity of host '192.168.122.10 (192.168.122.10)' can't be
established.
RSA key fingerprint is c3:11:15:ae:5d:15:09:77:31:3c:fb:ce:de:5c:0f:d8.
Are you sure you want to continue connecting (yes/no)? yes
Warning: Permanently added '192.168.122.10' (RSA) to the list of known
hosts.
root@192.168.122.10's password:
Now try logging into the machine, with "ssh root@192.168.122.10", and
check in:

  ~/.ssh/authorized_keys

to make sure we haven't added extra keys that you weren't expecting.
```

At this point we should be able to SSH into the virtual machine we created earlier without any prompt for passwords. Onward and upward, let's do some interactive commands to get a feel for what Ansible can do and what we can do with Ansible. First, we will need to modify either the default configuration file for the Ansible host inventory or create a temporary one. The default is located at `/etc/ansible/hosts` and it contains some examples of how hosts can be expressed using some globing and ranges in fields, but for now we will use a temporary host file so as to not disturb the one on the system, and also to show how to use a custom hosts inventory. Create a file in the home directory of the user you've been working as by editing `~/ansiblehosts` with your favorite editor and placing inside it the following:

```
[brokers]
192.168.122.10

[nodes]
192.168.122.10

[support_nodes]
192.168.122.10
```

What we have done here is created three host groups, each with only one member assigned by IP. Now the single host in each host group happens to be the same IP since we'll be deploying all components of OpenShift Origin to the same machine. This is certainly not the extent of the functionality found within Ansible host files. As can be seen here, the hosts server inventory file is a simple **INI** file (`https://en.wikipedia.org/wiki/INI_file`), such that our host groups are contained within brackets, or are listed as "subjects" in INI vocabulary terms. All IP addresses or hostnames listed in the following code snippet are a host group name belonging to that group; we can have many hosts within a group specified by either an IP or DNS pointer. The following is an example snippet from the default `/etc/ansible/hosts` file that shows some of this capability:

```
# Ex 1: Ungrouped hosts, specify before any group headers.
#green.example.com
#blue.example.com
#192.168.100.1
#192.168.100.10


# Ex 2: A collection of hosts belonging to the 'webservers' group
[webservers]
alpha.example.org
beta.example.org
192.168.1.100
192.168.1.110


# If you have multiple hosts following a pattern you can specify
# them like this:
www[001:006].example.com


# Ex 3: A collection of database servers in the 'dbservers' group
[dbservers]
db01.intranet.mydomain.net
db02.intranet.mydomain.net
10.25.1.56
10.25.1.57


# Here's another example of host ranges, this time there are no
# leading 0s:
db-[99:101]-node.example.com
```

Alright, now that we have an understanding of the hosts files and have written our own, let's take Ansible for a quick spin, running some interactive commands using the groups we've defined in our example. The following command will use Ansible's `ping` module to make sure the machines within the specified group are accessible; of course we only have one machine for the sake of simplicity, but this will still help get the idea:

```
$ ansible brokers -m ping -i ~/ansiblehosts -u root
192.168.122.10 | success >> {
    "changed": false,
    "ping": "pong"
}
```

What we've done here is relatively simple in nature, but it has allowed us to communicate with all the servers within the `brokers` group that are listed in the `~/ansiblehosts` inventory file, using the `ping` module. We have told Ansible to use the `root` user with the `-u` parameter. We could have also specified `all` where we specified `brokers` so that every server within the inventory would have had the specified action run against them, but since we only have one server for our example, it would have been redundant. Next up we should do something a little more advanced. We'll perform this action in two ways to show off a little of the power of the simplicity, and also to show an example of a built-in module; the importance of built-in modules will become apparent shortly.

 The output of the following command has been modified for brevity, it will look similar but there is going to be more of it. This is expected. Also, if you have followed this guide step-by-step without running any other commands, you will see a warning about importing a GPG key from the Fedora Project, this is also normal and expected.

```
$ ansible brokers -m shell -a "yum -y install vim-enhanced" -i ~/
ansiblehosts -u root
192.168.122.10 | success | rc=0 >>
Loaded plugins: langpacks, refresh-packagekit
Resolving Dependencies
--> Running transaction check
---> Package vim-enhanced.x86_64 2:7.4.016-1.fc19 will be installed
--> Processing Dependency: vim-common = 2:7.4.016-1.fc19 for package:
2:vim-enhanced-7.4.016-1.fc19.x86_64
--> Processing Dependency: perl(:MODULE_COMPAT_5.16.3) for package:
2:vim-enhanced-7.4.016-1.fc19.x86_64
--> Processing Dependency: libperl.so()(64bit) for package: 2:vim-
```

```
enhanced-7.4.016-1.fc19.x86_64

--> Processing Dependency: libgpm.so.2()(64bit) for package: 2:vim-
enhanced-7.4.016-1.fc19.x86_64

---> Package vim-common.x86_64 2:7.4.016-1.fc19 will be installed

--> Processing Dependency: vim-filesystem for package: 2:vim-
common-7.4.016-1.fc19.x86_64

---> Package vim-filesystem.x86_64 2:7.4.016-1.fc19 will be installed

--> Running transaction check

--> Finished Dependency Resolution


Dependencies Resolved


===============================================================================
=======
 Package                  Arch       Version              Repository
Size
===============================================================================
=======
Installing:
 vim-enhanced             x86_64     2:7.4.016-1.fc19        updates
1.0 M
Installing for dependencies:
 vim-common               x86_64     2:7.4.016-1.fc19        updates
5.9 M
 vim-filesystem           x86_64     2:7.4.016-1.fc19        updates
9.1 k


Transaction Summary
===============================================================================
=======
Install  1 Package (+16 Dependent packages)


Total download size: 18 M
Installed size: 59 M
Downloading packages:
Public key for perl-Carp-1.26-243.fc19.noarch.rpm is not installed
Public key for gpm-libs-1.20.6-33.fc19.x86_64.rpm is not installed
-------------------------------------------------------------------------------
-------
```

```
Total                                          981 kB/s  |   18 MB
00:18
Retrieving key from file:///etc/pki/rpm-gpg/RPM-GPG-KEY-fedora-x86_64
Running transaction check
Running transaction test
Transaction test succeeded
Running transaction
  Installing : 2:vim-filesystem-7.4.016-1.fc19.x86_64
14/17
  Installing : 2:vim-common-7.4.016-1.fc19.x86_64
15/17
  Installing : 2:vim-enhanced-7.4.016-1.fc19.x86_64
17/17
  Verifying  : 2:vim-common-7.4.016-1.fc19.x86_64
10/17
  Verifying  : 2:vim-filesystem-7.4.016-1.fc19.x86_64
13/17


Installed:
  vim-enhanced.x86_64 2:7.4.016-1.fc19


Dependency Installed:
  vim-common.x86_64 2:7.4.016-1.fc19
  vim-filesystem.x86_64 2:7.4.016-1.fc19


Complete!
```

In the previous command we used Ansible to run a single command within a shell environment on the remote servers. There is another module known as command, which is similar but does not provide the shell environment so all paths need to be absolute. Next, we will utilize the yum module to perform the same action but without the need to write the raw command. Note the state field changed: true in the JSON output of the action; if we were to run the Ansible command again it would be altered to changed: false and this alteration relates to the previous mention about the fact that Ansible's orchestration is idempotent. A code snippet for this is as follows:

```
$ ansible brokers -m yum -a "pkg=vim-enhanced state=installed" -i
~/ansiblehosts -u root
192.168.122.10 | success >> {
```

```
    "changed": false,
    "msg": "",
    "rc": 0,
    "results": [
        "vim-enhanced-7.4.016-1.fc19.x86_64 providing vim-enhanced is
already installed"
    ]
}
```

These commands we have run are considered **tasks** and we are able to combine tasks using a very simple YAML syntax in order to create a playbook. Since we've written a couple of simple commands, let's put them together and make a simple playbook that we can execute and view some output from. One thing we're going to also do here is take the opportunity to introduce **Jinja2** (`http://jinja.pocoo.org/docs/`), the simple yet powerful open source templating tool that Ansible uses for templating file manifests.

Jinja2 is capable of a multitude of features including, but not limited to, variable substitution, conditionals, flow control, loops, template inheritance, and configurable syntax. Most of these we will not be discussing, but those who are interested in more advanced features should certainly visit the project's website in order to see all that Jinja2 has to offer. Now, in order to prepare ourselves for the Ansible playbook, we will need our template, which is going a to use simple variable substitution; so create a directory named `~/templates` and place the following contents inside a file located at `~/templates/example_template.j2`:

```
This template is awesome, we can do all kinds of fun configuration with
it:


# Variables starting with the name ansible_ are supplied by "facts"
# that the ansible 'setup' module
My IP Address is: {{ ansible_default_ipv4.address }}


# This variable is set in our playbook
My custom configuration parameter is: {{ my_config_param }}
```

With the template in place, we can now write our simple example YAML-based Playbook which is as follows. We will take a moment to go through it step-by-step, so fear not if it looks slightly odd at first glance. This file should be named `example.yml`:

```
---
# This is an example Playbook
# #
- name: Example Play
  hosts: brokers
  user: root
  vars:
    my_config_param: some_config_parameter
    motd: "Ansible is awesome!"
  tasks:
    - name: Install vim-enhanced
      yum: pkg=vim-enhanced state=installed
    - name: Install my template
      template: src=templates/example_template.j2
                dest=/etc/example.conf
                owner=root group=root mode=0644 backup=yes
```

The very first line contains a series of three - characters, which is YAML syntax, for marking the "starting point" of a YAML document. After the initial line, we see the name of the current Play, the name designated to a set of combined actions within Ansible. A single Playbook may contain multiple Plays, but note that each one has its own variable scope and that order matters as Ansible will execute each Play, and the action within a Play, from top to bottom. Inside the Play named "Example Play" we defined the default set of hosts to run against within the `hosts:` directive, defined the default user to run the tasks within this playbook as with the `user:` directive, defined some variables needed for the tasks, and finally defined the tasks to be performed. The first task is a yum install and I've borrowed the example we've already run previously but wanted everyone to see it in action within a Playbook.

Finally our example playbook uses the templating engine to install a rather useless "configuration" file on the location `/etc/example.conf` on the remote system, but shows off a decent amount of the power this offers us. As we can see, the `template:` directive is the module in use here and we are providing it with the parameters of the template's source `src=` directive. We then define the destination location on the remote system of the file that, after having gone through interpretation using the templating engine, the file should be located and it is defined with the `dest=` directive. Then we provide the parameter's owner, group, and mode of the file in the location specified by the `owner=`, `group=`, and `mode=` directives. One last thing we've done is specified that we want Ansible to create a backup of a file on the remote system, if in the event it is pre-existing and would be modified by the Playbook. Alright, we should be ready to go, so let's run this thing!

> The command `ansible` is for ad-hoc server orchestration, whereas the command `ansible-playbook` is used for running predefined or preconfigured Playbooks, so be sure to take notice of that in the following example.

```
$ ansible-playbook example.yml -i ~/ansiblehosts


PLAY [Example playbook] ********************


GATHERING FACTS ********************
ok: [192.168.122.10]


TASK: [Install vim-enhanced] ********************
ok: [192.168.122.10]


TASK: [Install my template] ********************
changed: [192.168.122.10]


PLAY RECAP ********************
192.168.122.10                  : ok=3    changed=1    unreachable=0
failed=0
```

As we can see, each task ran, and since we've already installed vim-enhanced previously in the example, the task simply returned **ok**, which once again relates back to the idempotent nature of Ansible. I won't consume too much space with showing all of the output one more time, but we would see the following Play Recap, as the template would not make any modifications on a second or any subsequent run if we did not alter the template itself:

```
PLAY RECAP *********************
192.168.122.10                    : ok=3    changed=0    unreachable=0
failed=0
```

Alright, one more thing, let's inspect the file that was laid down, and just for the fun of it, let's use Ansible to do it!

```
$ ansible brokers -m shell -a "cat /etc/example.conf" -i ~/ansiblehosts
192.168.122.10 | success | rc=0 >>
This template is awesome, we could do all kinds of fun configuration with
it:

# Variables starting with the name ansible_ are supplied by "facts"
# that the ansible 'setup' module
My IP Address is: 192.168.122.10

# This variable is set in our playbook
My custom configuration parameter is: some_config_parameter
```

It can be observed that the template did exactly what we wanted it to do and installed the configuration file for us. Now, you may be asking yourself why this book went from OpenShift Origin to Ansible all of a sudden. Well, that's because it is one of the many ways that OpenShift can be deployed and happens to be your author's favorite of the bunch.

Before we move on, we need to understand one more concept of Ansible and that is what is called **roles**. A role in Ansible is meant to match up to the role in which a server plays in your environment. For example, a server is likely to be a web server, a database server, or a message queue server. Each of these things, and much more, can be considered a role of that server and a single server can perform many roles. The specific definition of roles configuration is outside the scope of this text as we won't need to write any roles from scratch, but simply understand the concept as it will be used in the next section. For more information on Ansible roles, please visit http://www.ansibleworks.com/docs/playbooks.html#roles.

The good news is we're not going to write an Ansible Playbook from scratch in order to deploy, but instead we will use the one that your author has written and at the time of this writing, I am working towards making it an official part of the OpenShift Origin upstream project.

Deployment

There are many options in deploying OpenShift Origin, all of which are documented at `http://openshift.github.io/`. The complete step-by-step guide to deploying OpenShift Origin by hand is maintained in the official documentation at `http://openshift.github.io/documentation/oo_deployment_guide_comprehensive.html`. However, for the sake of not reinventing an already well-designed wheel, we will not be covering deployment this way. We will be using Ansible for deployment of our OpenShift Origin environment, and the Ansible Playbook that we will use will be developed based on the procedures found in the official documentation. As a reminder, we will be using a single-node configuration such that all the components will be running on a single system, but there will still be a logical breakout of a Broker, Node, and Broker Support Nodes. The **Broker Support Node** is simply a logical breakout of services that the OpenShift Broker requires. This will become more clear as we look at the Ansible Playbook. The first step leading to deployment will be to clone the Git repository from GitHub containing the Ansible Playbooks.

The contents of this may change as development of the Playbook continues. Always consult the comments in the file we're about to edit as well as the `README.md` file found within the Git repository.

```
$ git clone https://github.com/maxamillion/ansible-openshift_origin.git
Cloning into 'ansible-openshift_origin'...
remote: Counting objects: 1171, done.
remote: Compressing objects: 100% (505/505), done.
remote: Total 1171 (delta 503), reused 1168 (delta 502)
Receiving objects: 100% (1171/1171), 176.85 KiB | 0 bytes/s, done.
Resolving deltas: 100% (503/503), done.
```

If, for any reason, there are portions of the Ansible playbook cloned from GitHub that are not functioning as expected or described in this text, please file an issue ticket so that it can be fixed at `https://github.com/maxamillion/ansible-openshift_origin/issues`.

We will then want to change directories so that our current working directory is `ansible-openshift_origin`. From there we should first take note of the `site.yml` file as it will give some insight into what roles each host group within our site are taking on. The following are the contents of the `site.yml` file at the time of this writing:

```
---
# This Playbook would deploy the entire OpenShift Origin environment

- hosts: all
  roles:
   - role: common

- hosts: support_nodes
  roles:
    - role: mongod
    - role: activemq
    - role: named

- hosts: nodes
  roles:
    - role: oo-node

- hosts: brokers
  roles:
    - role: oo-broker
    - role: oo-console
    - role: mcollective-client

- hosts: all
  roles:
    - role: post-deploy
```

Here we can see that each host group has a set of roles that they will fulfill within the Ansible Playbook. For all hosts we will want the role of `common`, which is simply common tasks needed on every server. We also have the `post-deploy` role that will perform simple cleanup and verification tasks where applicable. All other roles should look familiar from previous discussions of OpenShift architecture. Of course, for those curious about the details of the roles, I encourage you to poke around the `roles/` directory found within the Git repository and become familiar with the tasks involved.

We need to make a couple of edits before letting the magic happen, one of which is to the group_vars/all file and that is to set our DNS server's IP address. Open the file group_vars/all with the text editor of your choice and find the location of the oo_ns_server_ip variable and set it to 192.168.122.10, which is the IP we assigned to our virtual machine previously, as shown:

```
# oo_ns_server_ip - the DNS server that is authoritative for your
environment
#
oo_ns_server_ip: "172.16.0.8"
```

Next we need to decide whether we would like to deploy the latest stable version of OpenShift Origin or use the latest Nightly built RPM packages. We will be using the stable version for a consistent experience as the Nightly builds can sometimes contain unknown bugs. Edit the same file as before, group_vars/all, and find the section OpenShift Origin Version and edit it to reflect the following:

```
# OpenShift Origin Version - nightly or stable?
#
# You can technically set both to true, but because of the package
# versions oo_nightly will "win" at install/update time
#
# oo_stable - if set to true it must be paired with a
#             oo_stable_ver number, at the time of this writing
#             version 2 is most recent.
oo_nightly: "false"
oo_stable: "true"
oo_stable_ver: "2"
```

What we can do from this point is run the site.yml playbook and it will deploy the entire OpenShift environment for us.

 Some of this output is likely to vary as continued development efforts happen in OpenShift Origin, and the Ansible Playbook is updated to reflect these changes, as well as continued work on the Playbook to support more sophisticated deployments.

```
$ ansible-playbook site.yml -i ~/ansiblehosts -u root


PLAY [all] ************************************************************
******


GATHERING FACTS ******************************************************
******
```

```
ok: [192.168.122.10]


TASK: [Setup OpenShift Origin Nightly Repo] ****************************
******

skipping: [192.168.122.10]


TASK: [Setup OpenShift Origin Nightly Supplemental Repo]
***********************

skipping: [192.168.122.10]


TASK: [Setup OpenShift Origin Stable] *********************************
******

changed: [192.168.122.10]


TASK: [Setup OpenShift Origin Nightly Supplemental Repo]
*********************

changed: [192.168.122.10]


TASK: [SELinux Enforcing (Targeted)] **********************************
******

ok: [192.168.122.10]


TASK: [Ensure Installed - policycoreutils] ****************************
******

ok: [192.168.122.10]


TASK: [Ensure Installed - policycoreutils-python]
****************************

changed: [192.168.122.10]



... (omitted for brevity) ...


PLAY RECAP ************************************************************
******

192.168.122.10      : ok=136   changed=131   unreachable=0   failed=0
```

> There are a number of sections in the previous output that have been omitted, so we don't spend too much time staring at output that you also have on your computer screen. Those interested in the individual steps can easily consult the Playbook's contents.

Now that our deployment is complete, we can point our rhc client towards our newly installed OpenShift Origin platform as a Service Cloud environment, and use it just as we used the Online offering in *Chapter 2, Using OpenShift*. We can do this by running the same command we did in *Chapter 2, Using OpenShift*, in order to set up our rhc client, but now passing an argument in the server.

> At the time of this writing, the default username and password set up by the Ansible Playbook is username: demo and password: demo, but this could possibly change in the future so please consult the README.md file available in the Git repository.

```
$ rhc setup --server=192.168.122.10
OpenShift Client Tools (RHC) Setup Wizard

This wizard will help you upload your SSH keys, set your application
namespace, and check that other programs like Git are properly installed.

Login to broker.example.com: demo
Password: ****

Saving configuration to /home/user/.openshift/express.conf ... done

No SSH keys were found. We will generate a pair of keys for you.

    Created: /home/user/.ssh/id_rsa.pub
```

At this point we can use our `rhc` command-line tools in the same way we did with OpenShift Online in *Chapter 2, Using OpenShift*. We can also access the Broker REST API as we did with the OpenShift Online offering using the `curl` utility mentioned in *Chapter 3, OpenShift – Technologies and Working*:

```
$ curl -k -X GET \

  https://192.168.122.10/broker/rest/api
{"data":{"API":{"href":"https://openshift.redhat.com/broker/
rest/api","method":"GET","optional_params":[],"rel":"API entry
point","required_params":[]},"GET_ENVIRONMENT":{"href":"https://
openshift.redhat.com/broker/rest/environment","method":"GET","optional_
params":[],"rel":"Get environment information","required_params":[]}


... (omitted for brevity)...
```

It should also be noted that we used the IP address for the configuration and execution of the preceding example. However, if the client machine running the `rhc` clients and `curl` utility were to point to the Broker, which is now running a Bind DNS server (named), the fully qualified domain names could instead be used, such as `broker.example.com`.

Summary

In this chapter we have discussed DevOps, the Fedora Project, and OpenShift's relationship with Fedora. From there we deployed Fedora to a virtual machine using open source virtualization tools. We covered the topic of using Ansible as an orchestration and configuration management utility and used it to deploy OpenShift to our Fedora virtual machine. Finally, we configured our `rhc` command-line utility to point to our newly installed OpenShift Origin environment so that we may utilize it, and showed how to use the REST API with our OpenShift Origin environment. Hopefully we've all had a lot of fun and are now hacking on our very own open source PaaS with ease, and have a better understanding of all the technologies and utilities that are combined to make it all a reality. As always, visit `https://openshift.com` for the latest on OpenShift news. Happy hacking!!

Index

Symbols

-u parameter 86

A

ActiveMQ
  URL 64
ADD APPLICATION option 46
addon cartridge 36
Ansible
  about 76, 82-92
  URL 12, 82
ansible-playbook command 82
AnsibleWorks
  URL 82
Apache CloudStack
  URL 11
Application 64, 65

B

backports 77
Bcfg2
  URL 12
Broker, OpenShift 24
Broker Support Node 93

C

Cartridge 24
cd myawesomewebapp command 30
cgroups 61, 62
Chef
  URL 12
CLI
  about 29

  using 29-44
Client tools
  about 23
  Broker 24
  Node 24
cloud
  Git 16-21
  IaaS 10-12
  PaaS 12, 13
  SaaS 13
  SSH 14, 15
Command-Line Interface. *See* CLI
Continuous Integration (CI) 39
control groups. *See* cgroups
ctl_all command 43
ctl_app command 43
curl command 71, 72
curl utility 69, 73

D

DevOps 12

E

Eucalyptus
  URL 11
export command 43

F

Fedora Documentation Project
  URL 78
Fedora Project
  about 76-81
  URL 76

Thank you for buying
Implementing OpenShift

About Packt Publishing

Packt, pronounced 'packed', published its first book "*Mastering phpMyAdmin for Effective MySQL Management*" in April 2004 and subsequently continued to specialize in publishing highly focused books on specific technologies and solutions.

Our books and publications share the experiences of your fellow IT professionals in adapting and customizing today's systems, applications, and frameworks. Our solution based books give you the knowledge and power to customize the software and technologies you're using to get the job done. Packt books are more specific and less general than the IT books you have seen in the past. Our unique business model allows us to bring you more focused information, giving you more of what you need to know, and less of what you don't.

Packt is a modern, yet unique publishing company, which focuses on producing quality, cutting-edge books for communities of developers, administrators, and newbies alike. For more information, please visit our website: www.packtpub.com.

About Packt Open Source

In 2010, Packt launched two new brands, Packt Open Source and Packt Enterprise, in order to continue its focus on specialization. This book is part of the Packt Open Source brand, home to books published on software built around Open Source licences, and offering information to anybody from advanced developers to budding web designers. The Open Source brand also runs Packt's Open Source Royalty Scheme, by which Packt gives a royalty to each Open Source project about whose software a book is sold.

Writing for Packt

We welcome all inquiries from people who are interested in authoring. Book proposals should be sent to author@packtpub.com. If your book idea is still at an early stage and you would like to discuss it first before writing a formal book proposal, contact us; one of our commissioning editors will get in touch with you.

We're not just looking for published authors; if you have strong technical skills but no writing experience, our experienced editors can help you develop a writing career, or simply get some additional reward for your expertise.

open source*
community experience distilled

OpenNebula 3 Cloud Computing

ISBN: 978-1-84951-746-1   Paperback: 314 pages

Set up, manage and maintain your Cloud and learn solutions for datacenter virtualization with this step-by-step practical guide

1.   Take advantage of open source distributed file-systems for storage scalability and high-availability

2.   Build-up, manage and maintain your Cloud without previous knowledge of virtualization and cloud computing

3.   Install and configure every supported hypervisor: KVM, Xen, VMware

Google Apps: Mastering Integration and Customization

ISBN: 978-1-84969-216-8   Paperback: 268 pages

Scale your applications and projects onto the cloud with Google Apps

1.   This is the English language translation of: Integrer Google Apps dans le SI, copyright Dunod, Paris, 2010

2.   The quickest way to migrate to Google Apps - enabling you to get on with tasks

3.   Overcome key challenges of Cloud Computing using Google Apps

Please check **www.PacktPub.com** for information on our titles

OpenStack Cloud Computing Cookbook

ISBN: 978-1-84951-732-4   Paperback: 318 pages

Over 100 recipes to successfully set up and manage coverage of Nova, Swift, Keystone, Glance, and Horizone

1. Learn how to install and configure all the core components of OpenStack to run an environment that can be managed and operated just like AWS or Rackspace

2. Master the complete private cloud stack from scaling out compute resources to managing swift services for highly redundant, highly available storage

3. Practical, real world examples of each service are built upon in each chapter allowing you to progress with the confidence that they will work in your own environments

Apache CloudStack Cloud Computing

ISBN: 978-1-78216-010-6   Paperback: 294 pages

Leverage the power of Cloudstack and learn to extend the CloudStack environment

1. Install, deploy, and manage a cloud service using CloudStack

2. Step-by-step instructions on setting up and running the leading open source cloud platform CloudStack

3. Set up an IaaS cloud environment using CloudStack

Please check **www.PacktPub.com** for information on our titles

www.ingramcontent.com/pod-product-compliance
Lightning Source LLC
Chambersburg PA
CBHW060157060326
40690CB00018B/4151